THE WHY CODE

THE WHY CODE

Santosh Surpure

Available on amazonkindle

Worldwide Published by

Pendown Press
PREMIUM BUSINESS PUBLISHER

PENDOWN PRESS LLP

An ISO 9001 & ISO 14001 Certified Co.,

Regd. Office: 3767A, Kanhaiya Nagar,
Tri Nagar, Delhi-110035

Ph.: 8130886000, 9650072927, 8595249536

E-mail: info@pendownpress.com

Branch Office: 1A/2A, 20, Hari Sadan, Ansari Road,
Daryaganj, New Delhi-110002

Ph.: 011-45794768

Website: PendownPress.com

Edition: 2026

Price: ₹ 399

ISBN: 978-93-7217-178-5

Layout and Cover Designed by Pendown Graphics Team

Dedicated to my family whose love shaped my values.
And to all those seeking meaning across life's paths.
This book is for your journey.

Table of Contents

Introduction i

Chapter 1 The Search for Meaning 1

- Why must mankind have a meaning?
- Relatable examples of people who had success but failed in fulfillment.
- How purpose acts as the root cause of true happiness and resilience.
- Excercise

Chapter 2 Discovering Your "Why" in Life 15

- Practical approach for uncovering personal purpose
- Exercises: journaling, life timeline, identifying peak moments of joy, asking "Why?" five times.
- Story of someone who shifted life direction after discovering their "why."

Chapter 3 Purpose and Life 27

- How purpose shapes our day-to-day living.
- Turning ordinary routines into intentional practices.
- The difference between existing vs. truly living.
- Story: Someone who transformed from burnout → balance by aligning with purpose.

Chapter 4 Purpose and Money 53

- Money as a servant, not a master.
- How financial goals feel different when aligned with deeper meaning.
- Examples of philanthropists, but also ordinary people, using money for meaningful causes.
- Exercises: Defining your “money story” and aligning it with purpose.

Chapter 5 Purpose and Health 71

- Health as the fuel to live your purpose, not just an aesthetic pursuit.
- The link between mental, physical, and emotional well-being.
- Practices: mindfulness, exercise, rest as acts of service to your purpose.

Chapter 6 Purpose and Career 81

- The difference between a job, a career, and a calling.
- How purpose can turn work into passion.
- Stories of professionals who realigned careers with meaning.
- Exercises: Identifying values vs. job roles.

Chapter 7 Purpose and Relationships 93

- Building connections based on shared values.
- How purpose strengthens love, friendship, family, and community.
- The ripple effect: living your purpose inspires others around you.

Chapter 8 Living a Purposeful Life 103

- Integration of purpose across all aspects.
- Daily practices: gratitude, reflection, intentional planning.
- Purpose as a lifelong journey, not a one-time discovery.

Chapter 9 Walking Forward with Purpose 113

WHY
WHY

Introduction

It was a refreshing Saturday evening when our group of college friends reunited after 17 years, each one of us having built our lives in different cities.

Despite the distance and years apart, we managed to plan a cozy night, eager to reconnect and reminisce about old times. The evening unfolded beautifully, filled with laughter and heartfelt moments as we recalled our college days: late-night assignment cramming, vibrant annual events, and the countless memories that shaped us.

I was observing Shashi, a man who, from the outside, seemed to have all he wanted in life. He was working with one of the most admired financial companies as a Group Head, a beautiful home in New Delhi, a healthy bank balance, a salary in seven digits, and a family that adored his fast-forward success.

All of us admired his success too, and often said, "He's living the dream life." Yet, when I sat with him the next day at noon, away from the noise of his so-called flourishing life, career, and achievements, after a long, serious discussion, he confessed with a heavy heart,

"मुझे नहीं पता कि मैं अंदर से इतना खाली क्यों महसूस कर रहा हूँ। मैंने वो सब कुछ कर लिया जो मुझे करना चाहिए था, लेकिन फिर भी मुझे संतुष्टि नहीं मिल रही है।"

(I don't know why I feel so empty inside. I've done everything I thought I was supposed to do, but I still don't feel fulfilled.")

His words stayed with me for a long time. They reminded me of a truth that many of us ignore until life forces us to confront it:

Success without purpose feels meaningless.

We can gather wealth, build careers, stay healthy, and surround ourselves with people, but if we don't know why we are doing it all, something important will always be missing.

Purpose is that missing piece.

It is the anchor that keeps us steady when storms come and acts like the compass that points us in the right direction when we feel lost. Without purpose, money becomes just a piece of paper or numbers, careers become endless routines, health feels like just another thing, and relationships struggle to go deeper. But with purpose, everything changes in life. The same money becomes a source/tool to create impact, the same career becomes a meaningful journey, the same health routine becomes a celebration of life, and the same relationships flourish into bonds of true connection.

Think of the great visionaries, leaders, and change-makers we admire across the world. What truly sets them apart is not just their intelligence or resources, but their sense of purpose. That inner fire gave them strength and courage to bounce back from failure, courage in adversity, and clarity in chaos.

While history celebrates their greatness, purpose is not reserved only for a few extraordinary people. It is something each one of us can discover and live with.

Our lives are made up majorly of five different dimensions: our personal growth, finances, health, careers, and relationships. Purpose brings them all together into a life of meaning. It is the thread that connects who we are with what we do. And once we find it, we stop living on autopilot and start living intentionally.

This book is an invitation to that journey. It is not here just to hand you a step-by-step manual, because purpose cannot be given; it must be discovered.

Instead, it will offer stories, reflections, and insights that will help you pause, look deeper within, and uncover your own "why." It will show you how aligning your daily choices with your deeper meaning can bring joy, balance, and fulfilment into every area of your life.

So, as you turn these pages, I encourage you to ask yourself:

- What am I really living for?
- What impact do I want to create?
- How can my money, health, career, and relationships serve something larger than just comfort or convenience?

Because life is not measured by the number of years we live but by the depth of meaning we bring into each day.

Once you discover and know your purpose, every success will feel richer, every failure will feel like a lesson, and every moment will feel worth living.

This is your journey; not to chase more, but to live deeper. Not just to survive, but to thrive with purpose.

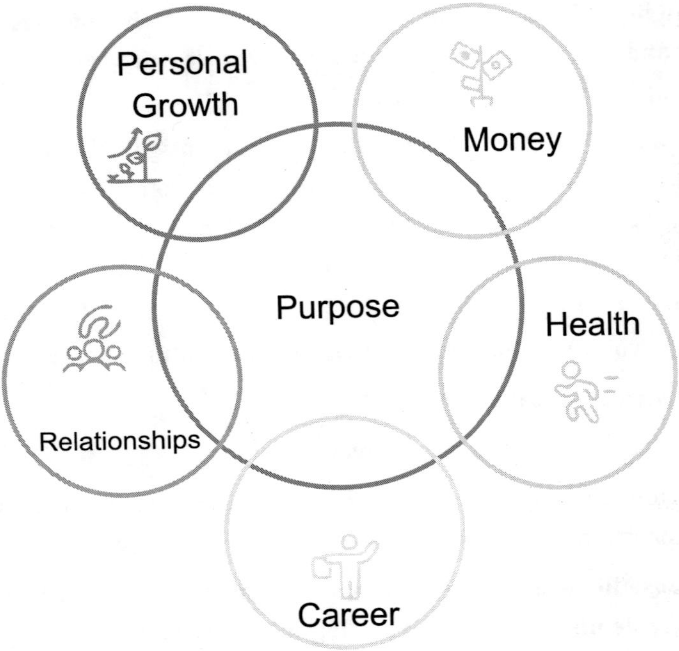
Personal Growth
Money
Purpose
Health
Relationships
Career

Chapter 1

The Search for Meaning: Navigating Life's Journey

The Fisherman and the Businessman

A Tale of Life's Wisdom & Purpose

There is a story often told about a simple fisherman living in a quiet coastal village.

Every morning, he went out in his small boat, caught just enough fish for his family, and returned home by noon. He spent his afternoon playing with his children, enjoying meals with his family, and relaxing with his friends under the shade of a tree.

His life was simple, yet deeply satisfying.

One day, a wealthy businessman visiting the village saw the fisherman returning, catching enough fish. Curiously, he asked, "Why don't you stay longer at sea and catch more fish?"

The fisherman smiled and replied, "I already have enough to provide for my family today."

The businessman persisted, "But if you caught more fish, you could sell them, earn more money, buy a bigger boat, and eventually own a fleet. Then you could open your own store, move to a big city, achieve bigger life goals, and one day, retire rich!"

The fisherman tilted his head and asked silently, "And after I retire rich, what would I do?"

The businessman laughed loudly, "You could spend your days relaxing with family, playing with your grandchildren, and enjoying life in peace."

The fisherman smiled again and said softly, "But that's exactly what I'm already doing."

This short yet simple story reminds us of an acute and deepest truth: chasing "more" without knowing why often leads us in circles.

The fisherman already had what the businessman was striving for—

- Purposeful living.
- A balanced life.
- And joy in the present moment.

Why We Crave Purpose

We, human beings, are driven by a need for meaning. From the earliest civilizations, we've sought stories, symbols, and beliefs that explain our existence. Ancient cultures created a series of myths about many things, not just to understand the stars or seasons, but to give our lives a sense of direction.

For centuries, philosophers have extensively studied the issue of purpose, and psychologists today have confirmed with various research that people who live with a strong sense of purpose enjoy greater resilience, health, and happiness.

Purpose is not just a philosophical idea; it's a biological need.

- When we feel our life has meaning and we start thinking and acting like that, our brains release various chemicals (dopamine, serotonin, norepinephrine, etc) that improve motivation, reduce stress, and strengthen our immunity.
- On the other hand, when we lack meaning, regardless of how much we succeed and achieve, we just flow and are more likely to fall short and get numbed by distraction.

A Deep Dive into the Human Need for Meaning

Humans are motivated by an inborn need for meaning, which influences our behaviors, ideas, and social structures. This craving for purpose is a basic aspect of who we are and transcends our ambition or survival. Our search for meaning has shaped our understanding of life from ancient times to the present, giving our lives direction and meaning. This section explores the causes of this craving, its biological and psychological bases, and its vital function in maintaining human health.

➢ The Historical Drive for Meaning

Since ancient times of humanity, people have sought ways to make sense of their place in the world. Early societies created stories and rituals to explain the mysteries of life through them, from the movement of the stars to the cycles of the seasons. These narratives provided more than answers to practical questions. They gave individuals and communities a sense of direction, a reason to exist, and a meaning to our lives. Whether through shared ceremonies or oral traditions, these early frameworks helped us to feel connected to something greater, anchoring lives with purpose.

This quest for meaning has persisted through the ages.

Thinkers across cultures, across the globe have studied and researched what makes life worthwhile, exploring questions of existence and fulfillment. Today, this search takes new forms: pursuing a meaningful career, nurturing relationships, or contributing to society, but the core impulse remains the same: "to live a life that feels significant."

➢ The Psychological Power of Purpose

A sense of purpose is vital to mental and emotional health. When people feel their lives have meaning, they tend to be more resilient, experiencing greater satisfaction and stability.

Purpose acts like an internal compass, helping individuals navigate challenges by giving them a reason to keep going.

For instance, someone who views their work as part of a larger mission, whether raising a family, creating something new, or helping others, can often endure setbacks with greater strength than those who feel their efforts lack impact.

Without purpose, people may feel adrift, trapped in a state of emptiness.

This can lead to disengagement, anxiety, or a tendency to seek distractions through excessive consumption or fleeting pleasures. Even achieving wealth or status can feel unsatisfying if it's not tied to a deeper sense of meaning. This disconnect often surfaces during moments of reflection, when people realize their accomplishments haven't brought the fulfillment they expected.

- **Purpose in the Modern World**

In today's fast-paced, interconnected society, the pursuit of meaning becomes more urgent and more elusive. Although many of our basic requirements have been satisfied by technological advancements and resource accessibility, feelings of alienation and discontent are frequent. It can be overwhelming to choose among so many options for vocations, lives, and beliefs, making it challenging to determine what is most important.

Continuous exposure to romanticized depictions of achievement can further worsen feelings of inadequacy and obstruct the search for meaning.

At the same time, traditional sources of meaning, such as close-knit communities or shared belief systems, have become less central for many. This shift places the responsibility of finding purpose on individuals, which can feel liberating but also frustrating. The result is a world where people may struggle to define their "why," turning to temporary distractions to fill the gap.

Yet, the modern era also offers unique opportunities to discover purpose. Technology connects us to causes and communities worldwide, allowing us to contribute to something larger than ourselves. Whether through creative pursuits, volunteering, or advocating for change, individuals can find meaning in many ways that resonate with their values.

- **Practising & Cultivating Purpose in Everyday Life**

  Finding purpose doesn't require dramatic changes or profound revelations in our lives. Often, it's about making small, intentional choices that align with what matters most for us. Reflecting on personal values, building meaningful relationships, or contributing to others' well-being can all foster a sense of purpose. Exploring new interests or taking on challenges can also reveal passions that give life direction.

Purpose is unique to each person.

For some, it might mean nurturing loved ones; for others, it could involve creating, learning, or making a difference in the world. What matters is the feeling that our actions have an impact, connecting us to a bigger story.

Success Without Purpose feels meaningless, as illustrated by the real-world examples shared below

Rahul- The Corporate Climber

Rahul was a corporate executive who worked tirelessly to climb the career ladder. By his mid-thirties, he had everything his younger self had dreamed of: a high salary, a stylish car, and a luxury apartment. But despite it all, he often found himself lying awake at night, feeling restless and unsatisfied.

All his hard work had given him money, but it hadn't given him meaning.

Madhu - The Entrepreneur

Madhu dedicated years to building her dream business. Her hard work paid off, her company grew rapidly, and society praised her as a "self-made success." Yet, when she finally took a moment to breathe, she confessed to a close friend,

"I feel like I've been running on a treadmill, moving fast, but going nowhere."

Rohan -The Fitness Enthusiast

Rohan spent hours in the gym, counting calories and tracking every workout. He looked fit from the outside, but deep down, he realized he was chasing health only for appearance.

His body was strong, but his spirit was exhausted.

It wasn't until he reframed health as a way to have energy for his passions and family that fitness truly became fulfilling.

Alia - The Social Butterfly

Alia loved being surrounded by friends, parties, and social media attention. But in her quiet moments, she often felt lonely.

She realized her relationships were wide but shallow, driven by convenience, not shared meaning.

When she started investing in deeper bonds built on trust and values, her sense of connection transformed.

The Hidden Truth of Lottery Winners

A study once followed people who suddenly became millionaires after winning the lottery.

- Surprisingly, it was found that many of them were less happy a year later than they were before.
- Why? Because money without a sense of purpose quickly loses its magic.
- Some misused it, some isolated themselves, and many admitted they wanted direction more than money.

These stories are not unique. They echo in the lives of millions of people who chase external markers of success, only to realize that achievement without alignment feels empty. 'Purpose' is that missing component that turns success into fulfillment.

Purpose as the Root of Happiness and Resilience

So, why does purpose matter so much?

Because it answers the deepest questions we all carry,

- "Why am I here?"
- "What impact can I create?"

- "What makes my life meaningful?"

When life is guided by purpose:

- Happiness is no longer dependent only on situations; it comes from within.
- Challenges become stepping stones, not roadblocks.
- Success feels significant because it contributes to something larger than ourselves.

Purpose doesn't eliminate struggles, but it gives us the strength to conquer them. Think of people who survive the toughest adversities, whether it is natural disasters, illnesses, or personal tragedies. Often, what keeps them going is not material wealth or external success, but a deep reason to live, a child to care for, a dream to pursue, a cause to fight for. Purpose becomes the anchor that holds them steady amidst the storm.

Psychologist Viktor Frankl, a Holocaust survivor, wrote in his classic book Man's Search for Meaning:

"Those who have a 'why' to live, can bear almost any 'how.'" His words reflect the universal truth: when you know your "why," you will find the courage to overcome any challenge.

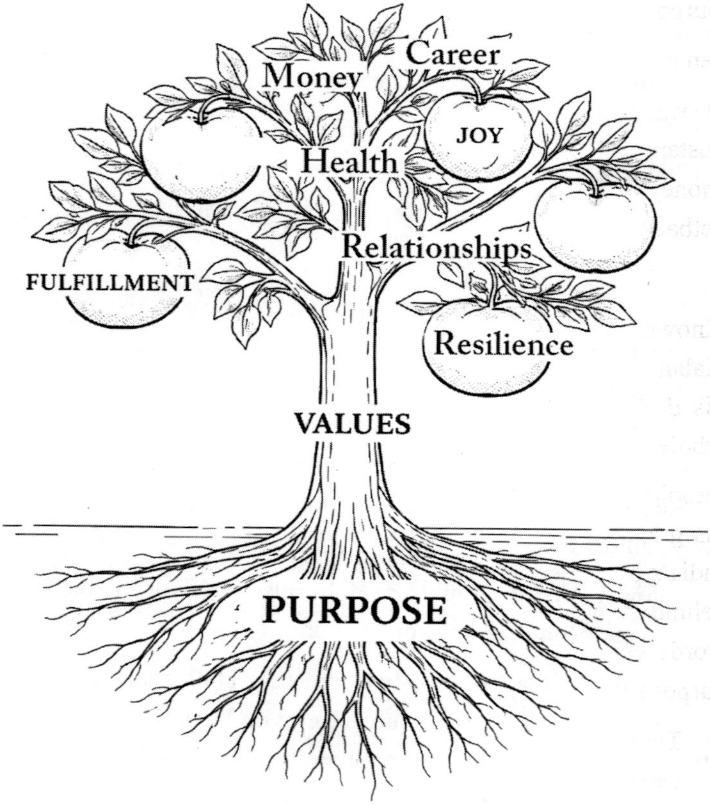

Real-Life Inspirations

Steve Jobs, Purpose as Innovation

Steve Jobs was not driven only by wealth or status; his purpose was to "make a dent in the universe."

For him, creating Apple wasn't just about building computers; it was about transforming the way people interact with technology.

Even when he was ousted from his own company, his sense of

purpose didn't fade away; it fueled him to create Pixar and later return to revolutionize Apple once again.

It was his purpose that guided him in decision-making and sustaining during difficult times, rather than being driven by money or status. His story shows how purpose sustains us during setbacks and fuels innovation that impacts generations.

Dr. A.P.J. Abdul Kalam, Purpose as Service

Known as the "Missile Man or People's President" of India, Dr. Kalam lived a life anchored in purpose, serving the nation with his deep knowledge of science and education, and inspiring the whole nation with his vision.

Despite global recognition, he lived a simple life, often saying his greatest joy came from igniting young minds. His vision for India's progress was not rooted in his personal gain but in leaving behind a legacy of empowerment and knowledge. Even today, his words inspire millions because they came from a deep sense of purpose.

- These examples remind us that purpose is not about fame, wealth, or recognition; it's about impact on society.
- And whether we touch the lives of millions or just a few around us, living with purpose makes our life journey meaningful.

Discovering Where Purpose Is Missing in Your Life

The question is not whether purpose is important or not; it is. The real question is whether we have allowed ourselves to pause and reflect on it. In the midst of the daily hustle, we all too frequently mistake busyness for purpose. However, being busy is not equivalent to having a purpose.

Take a moment to reflect:

- You may be earning well, but do you feel your money is serving a deeper cause in your life?
- You may be fit and healthy, but is your health helping you to live a more meaningful life, or is it just about looking good physically?
- You may be in a good relationship, but does it foster your growth, or is it just convenient?
- You may have built a career, but does it align with your core values in life, or is it draining your spirit?

If you deep dive with these kinds of questions may feel uncomfortable, but they are the beginning of clarity. Creating awareness is the first step toward transformation.

Exercise: A Personal Check-In

To end this chapter, take out your personal journal and pen. Sit alone in a quiet place for about 30 minutes or more, deep dive into your life lived till now, and ask yourself:

1. When was the last time I felt truly alive? What was I doing, and why did it touch my heart so much?
2. In which areas of my life (money, career, health, relationships, or personal growth) do I feel a sense of emptiness or restlessness?
3. What would I still choose to do if expectations from society, family, friends, and external expectations were removed? Would it still seem meaningful?
4. What kind of legacy do I wish to leave on other people's lives?

Whatever comes to your mind at first instance, write answers in a journal, without overthinking.

Don't worry if you don't have clear thoughts yet; the act of asking these questions itself is the beginning of discovering your own WHY.

To Sum It Up

We all need to look for meaning; it is not a luxury that only philosophers and saints can afford. Without it, life becomes a list of achievements without happiness. It makes even the most mundane activities - eating with loved ones, lending a hand to a stranger, or chasing a dream-rich with meaning.

This chapter serves as an invitation for you to take stock, examine yourself, and start the process of rediscovering your "why." Because everything else, including your finances, relationships, profession, and health, will take on a more profound and satisfying dimension after you discover it.

Chapter 2

Discovering Your WHY!

The Mountain That Wasn't His

There was once a man known for his ambition and discipline.

From a young age, he set his sights on the highest mountain in the world. To him, reaching its summit meant victory, to be known as the man who climbed the mountain.

For years, he trained relentlessly. He sacrificed comfort, relationships, and ease.

When the expedition finally began, it demanded everything from him: months of preparation, grueling climbs, oxygen-thin air, relentless cold, and constant danger.

Many times, turning back would have been the wiser choice, but he pressed on.Against all odds, he reached the summit.

Standing at the highest point on Earth, he planted his nation's flag, straightened his posture, and gazed out over the vast horizon below. This was the moment he had imagined for years. This was supposed to be fulfillment.

But instead of triumph, he felt an unexpected emptiness.

There was no joy. No deep sense of arrival. Only silence.

Years later, reflecting on that moment, he admitted something that surprised everyone who admired him:

"After years of climbing the mountain, I discovered that it wasn't my mountain."

- He realized that he had spent his life chasing a goal defined by applause, comparison, and expectation, rather than by his own values and calling.
- The climb had been real. The effort had been immense. But the purpose had never truly been his.
- That is the danger of living life without a deeper why.
- You may achieve your goal, you may succeed, you may even impress others and the external world, but deep inside, you will feel the quiet sting of misalignment of life.
- Purpose, or the reason behind our activities, is not merely a philosophical or spiritually aspirational concept. It serves as life's compass or north star. It provides us with direction, supports us throughout our difficult times, and guarantees that our accomplishments truly offer fulfillment rather than emptiness. Without it, we run the risk of leading lives that are without purpose and impact.

What Is a "WHY"?

You must have observed that many times we wake up in the morning full of energy, get ready for the day with enthusiasm, and complete all scheduled activities well within time with a smile on our face, and sometimes it goes exactly opposite to it, and we start the day feeling drained……

Your "Why" is the reason behind it.

The "why" is the reason you wake up in the morning with energy instead of dread. It is the energy that gives meaning to your hardships. It's what makes your accomplishments and setbacks meaningful.

Simon Sinek, in his famous **TED Talk and book Start with Why,** explained that people and organizations who succeed at the highest level all have a clear why. Apple didn't just sell computers, its why was to "challenge the status quo while empowering individuals with technology."

Mahatma Gandhi didn't just lead India's independence movement; his why was rooted in a commitment to truth and non-violence as a path to justice.

Your why is not about what you do or how you do it; it's about why you do it. For example,

- You may be a teacher, but your why might be to ignite curiosity in young minds.
- You may be a businessperson, but your why could be to create opportunities for others.
- You may be a parent, but your why could be to help your kids grow up to be kind and strong people."

Without knowing your why, life feels like an unresolved puzzle game. With it, every action becomes part of a meaningful story.

Finding a WHY - Leading Personalities Edition

Sometimes discovering purpose happens dramatically, other times it unfolds slowly, like a new day beginning at the edge of the sky

Steve Jobs

During his famous 2005 commencement address at Stanford University, Jobs shared how facing death after a cancer diagnosis gave him clarity. He said,

"Remembering that you are going to die is the best way I know to avoid the trap of thinking you have something to lose."

His why was not simply building products, but creating tools that allowed people to unleash their creativity.

Dr. A.P.J. Abdul Kalam

Known as India's "Missile Man,"

Kalam's purpose went far beyond science and defence.

His deeper why was to ignite the dreams of India's youth and inspire them to build a stronger nation together.

He lived his why until his very last breath, passing away while delivering a lecture to students.

Sudha Murthy

As an engineer and philanthropist, her why has consistently been service.

Whether supporting rural education, women's empowerment, or healthcare initiatives, her work stems from a deep belief that knowledge and resources should be used to uplift society and those in need.

Finding a WHY - The Common Person Edition

Anita, the Teacher

Anita taught mathematics in a small-town school. At first, she thought of it as just a job.

But over time, she realized that her why was not about equations and exams; it was about building confidence in students who believed they weren't good enough.

That shift turned her from a routine instructor into a life-changing mentor for hundreds of children.

What do these stories have in common? They show that when people connect with their purpose of life, they stop working just for building wealth, recognition, or security. Their actions gain depth, their struggles gain meaning, and they are outlived by their legacy.

Discovering Your WHY

Finding your why is not about inventing something new. It's about uncovering what is already within you.

Here are a few practical frameworks to begin this journey:

1. **The Childhood Clues:** Think back to when you were a child. What activities lit you up? What drew your attention naturally? Often, our purest passions show up before the outside world tells us what we "should" do.
2. **The Energy Test:** Notice what activities make you feel most alive. Even when they are challenging, you leave them with more energy than before. That's a strong indicator of alignment with your why.
3. **The Perspective of Contribution:** Ask yourself: If I could use my strengths to solve one problem in the world, big or small,

what would it be? Purpose often lies at the intersection of what we are good at and what the world needs.

4. **The Eulogy Exercise:** Imagine your 80th birthday. Friends and family are giving speeches about your life. What would you want them to say? What legacy do you want to leave behind? This way of thinking helps us ignore the small, unimportant things and focus on what really counts

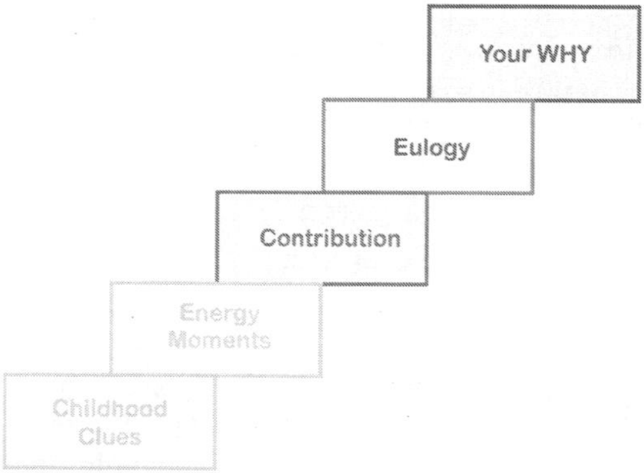

The Cost of Not Knowing Your WHY

Now, let us pause and reflect on the other side of the coin: what happens when we don't know our why?

Imagine a ship without a compass. It may travel thousands of miles, but without direction, it will drift endlessly, never reaching a meaningful destination. That is the cost of living without purpose.

1. Success Without Fulfillment

One of the most painful realities is that you can win and still feel like you've lost. Many people achieve what society defines as "success" - money, status, recognition & awards, yet feel restless inside.

Take Rajesh, a banker who climbed the corporate ladder. He lived in a luxury apartment and drove a premium car. Yet, one day, he admitted,

"I've been running for years, but I don't even know what I'm running toward."

Success without purpose is like eating food without tasting it. It fills you, but it doesn't satisfy you.

2. Burnout and Restlessness

Without a why, work becomes a race for "more": more money, more recognition, more possessions. But "more" is a finish line that keeps moving. People burn out not because they work too hard, but because they work without meaning.

Think of Aarti, who switched jobs every year. At first, she felt excited, but soon the same emptiness returned.

She wasn't chasing passion; she was chasing escape.

Purpose could have turned her career into a calling, but without it, it was just endless hopping.

3. Emptiness Despite Comfort

We live in an age of comfort, yet anxiety and depression are higher than ever. Why? Because comfort is not the same as fulfillment. Purpose is what transforms ordinary days into meaningful ones. Without it, even luxury feels hollow.

4. Shallow Relationships

Relationships built without shared meaning often feel transactional. You may live under the same roof, but feel like strangers. Purpose adds depth- it gives couples, families, and friends a shared vision. Without it, relationships sail like boats without anchors.

5. Fragility in Crisis

People who don't know why often fall apart when faced with hardship. They get hopeless and wonder, "Why me?" But people who have a purpose persevere in a different way. They perceive a purpose to continue even though they may suffer. The renowned and inspiring quote of Swami Vivekananda reads, "Arise, awake, and stop not until the goal is reached." This encourages having a strong purpose and continuing to strive, no matter the challenges.

6. Wasted Potential

Potential that is lost could be the biggest expense. Every person has gifts, but they are dormant if they are not used. Consider the innumerable tales that were never told, the innovations that were never made, and the acts of kindness that were never performed—all because people never found their purpose.

Bronnie Ware, a nurse who worked with the dying, wrote in her book that the top regret people shared was: "I wish I had lived a life true to myself, not what others expected of me." That is the ultimate cost of not knowing your why.

Integrating Purpose Into Daily Life

Discovering your why is only the first step; the true power of purpose lies in weaving it into everyday living. Purpose is not about waiting for a grand stage -it's about how you show up in your work, your relationships, your definitions of success, and even in your small daily habits. Let's explore how film stars have integrated purpose into their lives, and how you can too.

1. Align Your Work

In Bollywood, fame and money can come quickly, but lasting fulfillment comes when stars connect their work with their deeper why.

Take Amitabh Bachchan. At one point in his career, after a series of flops and financial challenges, and struggles, he could have walked away from the industry. Instead, he redefined his purpose, not just as an actor, but as a storyteller who inspires resilience and strength.

His comeback through Kaun Banega Crorepati was not just about reviving a career but it was about connecting with millions of ordinary Indians, giving them hope, courage, and a voice.

Today, he's respected not only for his talent but for the purpose and dedication he brings to his work.

Even if your job feels routine, connect it with your why. Your work becomes meaningful when you bring purpose into it, not when the title or role changes.

2. Shape Your Relationships

Purpose shines brightest in how we treat those closest to us.

Consider Shahrukh Khan (SRK). While he is celebrated as the "King of Bollywood," his purpose has always been rooted in love, relationships, and spreading joy.

He often speaks about how his mother's teachings shaped him, and despite superstardom, he prioritizes being present for his family. Beyond the spotlight, his strong bond and connection with fans are also built on this purpose.

He doesn't just entertain, he connects with emotions.

Whether it's his signature style open-arms gesture or his heartfelt speeches, he reminds people of the power of love and belonging.

When families or relationships align around purpose, whether it's love, growth, or service, they thrive. SRK is one of the living examples who shows us that purpose is not only about professional milestones, it's also about nurturing those bonds that define who we are and become a supermodel in society.

3. Redefine Success

Hollywood, too, has many stories of stars who had fame and money but still felt empty, until they redefined success.

Take Selena Gomez. She talked candidly about her battles with anxiety, sadness, and health issues at the prime of her career.

Even with international acclaim, she understood that achievement was lacking without personal peace. Her motivation became evident to remind others they are not alone and to normalize discussions about mental health. She later produced the documentary My Mind & Me and established the Rare Impact Fund to provide access to mental health care, demonstrating that genuine success is determined by one's alignment with their deeper why rather than by accolades or number-one hits.

Her journey inspires us to look beyond external validation.

A true measure of success is not "How much did I earn?" but "Did I move closer to what truly matters to me?"

4. Daily Check-In

Living with purpose is not about occasional grand gestures - it's about consistent daily choices.

Look at Bruce Lee. Well-known for his unparalleled self-control and discipline, he linked his daily schedule with his purpose to lead a balanced, developing, and contributing life.

He prioritized his mental clarity and physical condition, trained hard, and adhered to strict timelines. Beyond martial arts, he promoted concepts of harmony, inner power, and self-expression through his books and films. He considered whether his behaviors complemented his larger goal of encouraging others to reach their full potential every day in both his practice and his artwork.

His life is a reminder that daily check-ins don't need to be complex. A simple question like "Did I live my why today?" keeps us aligned, grounded, and moving in the right direction.

Living a Life of Alignment

When we look at film stars, it's easy to get dazzled by fame, money, and glamour. But their deeper journeys show us something universal:

Fulfillment doesn't come from applause; it comes from alignment.

- Amitabh Bachchan found purpose in resilience and connection.
- Shahrukh Khan, in love and relationships.
- Selena Gomez, in mental health advocacy.
- Bruce Lee, in discipline and contribution.

Each of them discovered that their true power came from how they matched their daily lives with their why, not from what the outside world offered them.

And the same applies to us. You don't need a stage, a camera, or millions of fans to live with purpose. All you need is the courage to align your work, your relationships, your success, and your habits with what truly matters to you.

Because when you do, life becomes a purposeful journey rather than merely a set of chores.

Questions For You To Reflect Upon

To close this chapter, go back to your personal journal, take a pause from your daily hustle for 30 minutes, and deep dive into your thoughts:

1. How can I bring my why into the work I do tomorrow?
2. Which relationships could grow stronger if I shared my why with them?
3. Am I defining success only by external achievements, or by alignment with my purpose?
4. Tonight, if I asked myself, "Did I live my why today?" What would my honest answer be?

Write your answers honestly. Clarity may not come instantly, but reflection opens the door.

To Sum it Up

The value of life is too great to be wasted aimlessly. Finding your why involves adding meaning to everything you already do, not making drastic changes all at once. Knowing your why transforms the ordinary into the extraordinary, challenges into opportunities for growth, and achievement into genuine fulfillment.

So, ask yourself, not tomorrow, not someday, but today: **"What is my why?"**

Because once you know it, your life will never feel the same again.

Chapter 3

Purpose and Life: Living with Intention

The Invisible Compass

Life often feels like a series of days strung together: wake up, work, eat, sleep, repeat. Yet, underneath this rhythm lies a deeper question: What is all of this for?

Purpose is that invisible compass guiding us, even when we are not aware of it. It influences our choices, our emotions, our resilience, and even our relationships.

Without a sense of purpose, daily routines can seem dull, like we are riders on a train traveling to an unknown destination. When driven by purpose, even the most basic tasks, such as nurturing a plant, assisting a coworker, or preparing a meal for loved ones, acquire a subtle yet significant significance.

Purpose does not typically come as a dramatic moment of clarity. Instead, it often unfolds gradually, much like the gradual illumination of dawn breaking over the horizon.

In this section, we will examine how purpose influences our everyday lives, transforming typical habits into meaningful practices, and how it differentiates simple survival from authentic living. And let's understand with an example of those who faced the challenges of burnout and found balance by reconnecting with their genuine purpose.

1. How Purpose Shapes Our Day-to-Day Living

When people think of purpose, they often imagine it as something grand: building a company, writing a bestselling book, or leading a movement. But purpose doesn't only live in extraordinary achievements, but it breathes inside the daily choices we make.

Consider two people starting their mornings.

→ One wakes up, scrolls through their cellphone, and drags themselves to work.

→ The other wakes up, hits the gym, whispers a small prayer or affirmation, and gets ready with the thought, "***Today, I get to contribute to something larger than myself.***"

Their tasks may be the same, emails, meetings, and chores, but the energy they bring into them is vastly different.

Purpose is not about what we do, but why we do it.

- A teacher who believes their purpose is to shape young minds approaches lessons differently from someone simply clocking in for a monthly salary.
- A doctor driven by purpose sees patients, not cases.
- A parent who cooks dinner out of love and care feels different from one who does it as an obligation.

In fact, purpose acts as a silent filter, coloring our experiences. When guided by purpose, obstacles become chances for development. Lacking that sense of purpose, even familiar comforts may seem empty…..

2. Turning Ordinary Routines into Intentional Practices

At first glance, daily routines may seem repetitive, even dull. Wake up, brush your teeth, make coffee, head to work, return home, prepare dinner, unwind, and sleep. Repeat the same tasks tomorrow. It can feel like a hamster wheel, continuously spinning.

But the 'magic happens' when we pause and ask: What is the purpose behind these actions?

Ordinary routines are not just mechanical habits; they are fertile ground for cultivating intentionality. When approached with awareness, they can become rituals that not only serve our needs but also nourish our deeper sense of meaning.

The Power of Intention

Intentionality is simply the act of bringing purpose into whatever we do. Imagine making a cup of tea in the morning. If you rush through it, it's just another task of the day. But if you pause, breathe in the aroma, and remind yourself that this tea is to energize and care for your body so you can show up fully for your day, the act becomes more than making tea. It becomes an expression of self-respect.

The same applies to exercise. Running on a treadmill while mindlessly watching television can feel like a task. But running while consciously repeating, "I am strengthening my body so I can live longer, love better, and serve deeper," shifts the activity into alignment with purpose.

Small Shifts with Big Impact

Consider how these small reframings change our everyday lives:

- **Cooking Dinner**
    - **Without purpose:** A tiring end-of-day obligation.
    - **With purpose:** An act of love, nurturing yourself or your family with nourishment.
- **Work Emails**
    - **Without purpose:** Endless tasks in an inbox that never seems to end.
    - **With purpose:** Communication that helps build bridges, solve problems, or support colleagues.
- **Morning Commute**
    - **Without purpose:** Frustrating traffic, wasted time.
    - **With purpose:** A window for podcasts, learning, or silence, a daily classroom on wheels.

When routines are aligned with a bigger "why," they no longer feel draining. Instead, they energize us.

Let's understand this with a few real-life examples

Mahatma Gandhi - Purpose in Simplicity

Mahatma Gandhi's life vividly illustrates how ordinary habits can be transformed into purposeful practices. He spun cotton every day on his Charkha (spinning wheel).

To an observer, this might have appeared to be a simple, even outdated activity. However, for Mahatma Gandhi, this act was profoundly intentional; it represented self-sufficiency, the dignity of work, and a stand against colonial oppression.

What many perceived as routine, Gandhi turned into a potent symbol of meaning.

Each turn of the wheel conveyed a message: A free India can be achieved through self-reliance. His daily task evolved into a ritual, and that ritual sparked a revolution.

Steve Jobs - Purpose in Design and Focus

It was well known that Steve Jobs wore the same black turtleneck every day. It appeared strange, even addictive, to many.

Jobs clarified that this was done on purpose in order to free up his energies for more important choices, such as creating things that would transform the world, by eliminating the daily dilemma of "What should I wear?"

In this case, a daily ritual (dressing) evolved into a deliberate effort to match his energy with his mission: to develop tools that foster human creativity.

Mary Kom - Purpose in Discipline

Mary Kom, the legendary Indian boxer, is another excellent example.

For her, exercising every day is about more than simply being physically fit. It's about fulfilling her job as an athlete and an inspiration to countless young girls.

Her early mornings, intense practice sessions, and rigid routines are not mere rituals; rather, they are deliberate actions that support her core "why," which is to demonstrate that women can succeed in any area despite all obstacles.

Her practice of rising early to train aims to create a movement of courage and hope rather than just muscle.

A Teacher's Story: Purpose in the Classroom

Not all examples come from famous personalities.

Consider the story of Rukmini Devi, a government school teacher in a small village in India.

Every morning, before beginning her class, she takes a few moments to silently bless her students, reminding herself: "My purpose is to shape lives, not just teach subjects."

Her students may never know about this ritual, but it changes how she teaches.

Lessons are no longer mechanical; they are alive with care and patience. This is how purpose transforms an ordinary act like writing equations on a blackboard into a practice of shaping futures.

The Ordinary as Sacred

Steve Jobs, co-founder of Apple, often emphasized that excellence lies in the details. He was known to care about aspects of product design that most people would overlook, even the inside of a computer, which no customer would ever see. To Jobs, crafting every detail with mindfulness was not trivial but sacred, because it reflected respect for the work itself.

He believed that even ordinary tasks, when done with presence and passion, could transform into something extraordinary.

For him, designing a button or refining a font was not routine work—it was an act of devotion to beauty and purpose.

Jobs's philosophy reminds us that ordinary acts, approached with awareness, can become powerful expressions of meaning.

The Ritualisation of Life

Routines become rituals when they are imbued with meaning. We are grounded by rituals. They give us purpose and serve as a reminder of our ideals.

Journaling every morning,

writing a gratitude note at the end of the day,

or lighting a lamp before work

These are not merely routines; they serve as daily reminders of the reasons behind our actions.

Finding remarkable events is not the goal; rather, it is about integrating the extraordinary into the everyday.

3. The Difference Between Existing vs. Truly Living

The distinction between simply existing and genuinely living is small yet significant. To exist is simply to go through the motions, waking, working, eating, and sleeping, without giving them much thought or purpose. But to truly live is to live with consciousness, passion, and a sense of belonging to something bigger than oneself. It's a pure act towards the desired goal of life to make a difference for the benefit of many lives or the surroundings.

Many individuals today live for years or even decades without realizing it. They live reactive lifestyles that are impacted by obligations, social conventions, and the external environment. Social standards may no longer affect our day-to-day activities or cause us to worry about how society may perceive our actions once we discover a purpose that leads and stabilizes us.

Existing: A Life on Autopilot

Imagine waking each morning with the same heaviness, dragging yourself to work you dislike, counting hours until the day ends, and then distracting yourself with television or scrolling endlessly through various social media platforms on your phone. Life becomes a cycle of survival, staying afloat, but not really thriving.

Existing is about our comfort zones, daily routines without meaning, and doing things simply because "that's what everyone does." It lacks vitality.

Truly Living: A Life With Fire Inside

Now, imagine waking with curiosity. Your work, even if hard, excites you because it aligns with something meaningful. Conversations feel alive. You notice the beauty of small moments and in many small stuff, the laughter of a child, the sunrise painting the sky, a kind word exchanged with a stranger, a little fragrance of flowers kept on the table.

Truly living is not about luxury or success. It's about alignment - when your actions, values, and goals resonate with your deeper "why." It is about becoming conscious and being fully awake in your own life.

Let's deep dive into it with a few real-life examples to understand it better

Mr. Ratan Tata: Finding Purpose Beyond Profit

There were a few business leaders who embodied the idea of living with purpose as deeply as Mr. Ratan Tata, the former chairman of the Tata Group.

Leading one of India's most respected conglomerates, he faced many challenges throughout his career while serving the nation in multiple areas of business that fulfilled the needs of not only India but across the globe. But it was not a cakewalk for him; it tested not only his business acumen but also his vision of what leadership truly means.

When the Tata Nano project, which became a top headline across the globe, faced criticism and setbacks, and even when Tata Motors acquired Jaguar Land Rover, one of the best conglomerates in the automobile industry, during a global recession, many doubted the decisions.

Yet Mr. Ratan Tata stood strong and firm on his decision, not because of short-term gains or losses but because he believed in a larger purpose: creating value, fulfilling dreams of the common man, preserving jobs, and giving India a respected place on the global business map.

For Tata, meaning was never about personal wealth.

His life's compass was to serve society, which he expressed through philanthropy in education, healthcare, rural development, and many other areas, which indirectly helped nation-building too.

He has often emphasized that "I don't believe in making the right decisions. I make decisions and then make them right." His resilience and clarity of purpose helped him as well as the organization to face criticism and emerge even stronger.

Mr. Ratan Tata's journey shows us that success is not measured only in profits but in the courage to pursue a vision that benefits others and leaves behind a legacy of trust.

Malala Yousafzai: Living for a Cause Larger Than Self

Malala Yousafzai's story is another well-known example. As a young girl in Pakistan, she could have simply existed within the limitations and social barriers placed upon her gender.

But she dared to truly live by standing up for the basic right of girls to receive an education in spite of having stricter social norms within the country and an inconducive environment for women.

Her purpose gave her courage even when she was shot by the Taliban. She not only survived but transformed her pain into power, becoming the youngest Nobel Peace Prize laureate.

While most of her age were simply "existing" in routines of school, social life, and family, Malala lived with fire, fueled by a cause that transcended her personal safety. Created a larger impact on society, due to her bold steps and unstoppable acts, today girls are getting an education and creating an impact on society, and helping the nation directly or indirectly.

Her story reveals that truly living is about being willing to take risks for something greater than oneself.

Mother Teresa: Purpose in Daily Service

Mother Teresa spent her life in service to the poorest of the poor.

For her, truly living was not about wealth, fame, or luxury. It was about finding Christ in the faces of the sick, the orphaned, and the dying.

Her daily routines, feeding the hungry, cleaning wounds, holding the hands of the dying, might seem ordinary acts of care. But because they were infused with purpose, they became sacred.

She reminds us that truly living doesn't always mean doing grand things. Sometimes, it means doing small things with great love.

The Common Thread

Across these stories, we see the same pattern:

- Existing is about survival.
- Truly living is about purposeful engagement.

The global personalities above, Tata, Malala, and Mother Teresa, show us that truly living is not about external conditions (wealth, freedom, power, or health) but about internal alignment with a "why."

Some lived in prisons, some faced bullets, some chose lives of poverty, and others chased impossible dreams. Yet all shared one trait: They were awake to their purpose, and that awakenedness turned existence into true life.

Ask yourself:

- Am I existing, or am I truly living?
- Do my daily actions align with a purpose bigger than myself?
- If I were to frame my routines in the light of purpose, how would they change?

4. From Burnout to Balance: Purpose as the Turning Point

The modern world often celebrates hustle, late nights, and endless work, and sacrifice in the name of ambition. Entrepreneurs in particular are seen as tireless machines, constantly pushing for innovating, building, and striving.

But beneath this glamorous life and glossy image lies a silent epidemic of **burnout.**

Burnout is the slow erosion of meaning, not just tiredness. It happens when the work that once inspired begins to feel like a burden, when the body rebels against the demands of ambition, and when the soul whispers, "Is this all worth it?"

Many entrepreneurs across the globe walked through this fire.

Their journeys reveal that balance is not found in slowing down alone, but in realigning with purpose.

Elon Musk: From Overdrive to a Life Anchored in Purpose

Elon Musk was a driven force in the mid-2000s, transforming industries with SpaceX and Tesla.

He was consumed with his goal to transform space travel and renewable energy, which resulted in unrelenting work schedules.

He frequently slept in offices or factories to meet deadlines, investor pressure, and engineering breakthrough demands. He was motivated, yet his life was a high-stakes race driven by objectives that provided little opportunity for introspection or equilibrium.

Musk reached a breaking point in 2008.

Tesla was on the verge of bankruptcy, SpaceX's early rocket flights had failed, and his personal life had collapsed due to a divorce and strained relationships.

He later said that this was one of the darkest times of his life, both mentally and physically. Not only was he professionally burdened by his near-failure, but it also had him face a more profound question: Why was he so driven?

Transformation was sparked by this calamity. Musk understood that even if his work was revolutionary, it needed a deeper foundation if it was solely used to achieve short-term objectives.

He started to reinterpret his life's mission as helping humanity's future rather than merely creating businesses.

In order to ensure the survival and growth of human consciousness, SpaceX set out to create multiplanetary life. In order to protect the environment for the next generations, Tesla exemplified a dedication to sustainable energy. These were more than just commercial endeavors; they served as his "why," a purpose that went beyond financial gain or social standing.

Musk reorganized his life with this newfound feeling of purpose rather than carrying on in overdrive.

In order to increase impact, he delegated duties, surrounded himself with teams that shared his vision, and concentrated on clarity. He prioritized high-leverage decisions while maintaining an aggressive work ethic, using techniques like first-principles thinking to keep his attention on what is really important. He set aside time for introspection to make sure his activities were in line with his ultimate objective, which was to make a positive, long-lasting impact on humanity.

This change started to show in his day-to-day activities. Musk balanced his drive with a dedication to long-term effect by adopting habits that kept him focused and energized.

He saw setbacks as chances to further his goals rather than as roadblocks. Tesla's ascent to prominence in sustainable energy and SpaceX's eventual successful launches served as examples of a life based on purpose rather than merely success.

What might have been a collapse turned into a breakthrough.

Musk was forced to face life's most profound questions by the chaos of 2008, which led him to a purpose that gave both his job and his existence tremendous significance. His experience demonstrates that finding meaning in life is about coordinating one's efforts with a bigger goal rather than running away from adversity. According to Musk, the real goal of life is to build a future in which mankind flourishes, demonstrating that a meaningful life can change both the individual and the world.

H.T. Parekh, Founder of HDFC: From Overdrive to a Life Anchored in Purpose

Throughout the 1950s and 1960s, H.T. Parekh played a significant role in India's financial scene, navigating the difficulties of a newly formed nation.

He worked tirelessly as a key member of ICICI to build a solid financial institution while juggling the demands of an expanding economy, legal requirements, and high-stakes decisions.

His days were occupied by meetings, strategic planning, and relentless efforts to establish credibility in a resource-constrained environment.

His life was a high-stress, ambition-driven marathon with little time for reflection or balance.

In the early 1970s, Parekh encountered a turning point. India's post-independence economic and bureaucratic challenges had a detrimental effect, in addition to the significant expense of establishing a financial institution.

He began to experience the physical and mental strain of his relentless pace as the weight of his role tested his resilience. This was more than just fatigue from work; it caused him to think more carefully about what was really motivating his relentless efforts.

Was he only building institutions, or did his labor serve a greater purpose?

This realization was the catalyst for transformation. Parekh saw that while his desire had an effect, it required a more solid basis founded on a meaningful objective.

Instead of focusing only on enhancing financial systems, he began to reframe his life's purpose as helping ordinary Indians achieve their goals. This goal was embodied in the founding of HDFC in 1977, a pioneering organization that aimed to make homeownership accessible through housing finance—a novel idea in a country where such opportunities were few. This was his "why," a goal to enhance people's lives and strengthen the ties of a developing nation; it was more than just a company.

With this newfound feeling of purpose, Parekh straightened his life rather than staying in overdrive. He concentrated on making things clear, assembling groups of people who shared his goal for financial inclusion, and assigning tasks wisely to have the maximum possible impact. He prioritized strategic choices that supported his objective while maintaining his unwavering devotion, leveraging his in-depth knowledge of economics and human needs to spur innovation. He set aside time for introspection to make sure his actions furthered his objective of giving the average person opportunities.

His daily behaviors began to reflect this shift.

Parekh struck a balance between his commitment to the welfare of society and his professional discipline by creating routines that kept him motivated and focused. Whether they were financial or legal, he viewed challenges as opportunities to achieve his objectives rather than as setbacks. Instead of just being an institutional accomplishment, the establishment and growth of HDFC, which enabled millions of people to become homeowners, came to represent a life with meaning.

What could have been fruitless became a breakthrough.

Parekh was pushed to confront life's deeper problems by the demands of the 1970s, which led him to a purpose that greatly enriched his life and career. His story demonstrates how, rather than striving to avoid hardship, it may be used to further a cause that benefits others in order to find meaning in life. Parekh's sincere goal was to lay the groundwork for a thriving, inclusive India by showing how a meaningful life can transform both the individual and society.

Anu Aga: From Corporate Pressures to Purposeful Philanthropy

As chairman of Thermax, one of India's leading energy and environmental companies, Anu Aga lived a life of extreme corporate responsibility. Managing a billion-dollar company involved numerous meetings, travel abroad, and constant pressure to deliver results.

Her true burnout, however, was both very personal and quite professional. When her husband and son unexpectedly died in the 1990s, she endured unbearable grief. The weight of sadness and business obligations may have shattered her spirit. Despite many people's anticipation that she would step down, she brought her pain into the boardroom.

For years, she led, accomplished, and functioned while living in survival mode after being hollowed out by grief.

The turning point came when she began asking deeper questions, including "What am I living for?" What does success really mean these days?

Her answers directed her toward philanthropy and social impact. After leaving Thermax, she dedicated herself to social issues, particularly education for the underprivileged, through organizations like Teach for India.

Her life changed from burnout to harmony when she embraced a goal bigger than herself, giving children the gift of education.

Change was now more important to her than corporate objectives.

She stated, "Life is about what you give back; it's not only about selfish gain."

The Common Thread: Purpose as the Healer

Despite coming from quite diverse backgrounds, Elon Musk in the West, Anu Aga & H T Parekh in India, their stories all lead to the same conclusion: burnout cannot be alleviated by rest alone. The answer lies in rediscovering meaning. While Anu's mission was to uplift people via social change and education, Parekh's mission was financial inclusion. Their routines changed. They had different definitions of success. Most importantly, their energy shifted from depletion to rejuvenation because purpose filled the well that burnout had drained.

Ask yourself:

- Where in your life are you "pushing through" without meaning?
- What loss, challenge, or burnout experience could actually be pointing you toward a deeper purpose?
- How might you redefine success, not just as achievement, but as alignment with purpose?

5. Practical Reflections: Bringing Purpose Into Daily Life

We have looked at how our days are shaped by our purpose, how everyday activities become sacred rituals, and how alignment with a "why" is what distinguishes actually living from merely existing. We have witnessed both Indian and international leaders who, by rediscovering their greater purpose, transformed burnout into equilibrium.

However, inspiration wanes if it is not put into practice. Purpose must permeate everyday life; it cannot exist solely in books or speeches. The good news? You don't have to make all the changes at once. All you have to do is begin modestly, mindfully, and purposefully.

Exercise 1: The Morning Purpose Check-In

- Each morning, before touching your so-called smartphone, pause for two minutes.
- Ask yourself: "Why am I living today? What is one way I can align with my deeper purpose in the next 24 hours?"
- Write down one word or phrase, such as "service," "creativity," "love," or "growth."
- Carry that word into your day like a compass.

Example: If your word is "service," you may respond to emails with more patience or help a colleague. If it is "growth," you may choose to learn something new on your commute.

Exercise 2: Turning Tasks Into Rituals

Take one mundane task you do daily, washing dishes, commuting, exercising, or cooking.

- **Step 1:** Pause before starting.
- **Step 2:** Name the deeper meaning behind it. ("I am cooking to nourish life." "I am exercising to honor my body.")
- **Step 3:** Perform the task slowly and consciously, remembering this meaning.

This simple reframing turns a "to-do" into a practice of purpose.

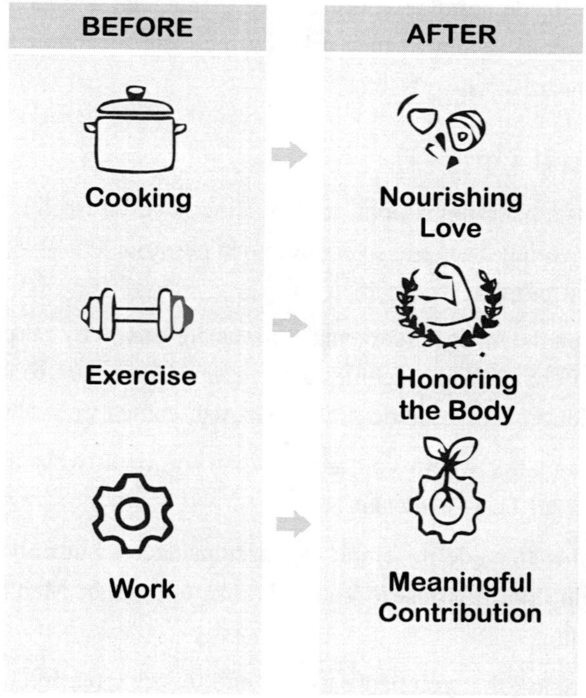

Exercise 4: The Burnout Compass

When you feel overwhelmed or empty, don't just push harder. Pause and ask:

1. What am I chasing right now?
2. Does it connect to my deeper purpose, or am I driven only by external pressure?
3. If I realigned with purpose, how would this task or goal look different?

Example: If you are overworking just for financial targets, but your deeper purpose is family, then ask how you can rebalance time and energy toward what truly matters.

To Sum it Up

Purpose is a path, not a Goal. It's not about waiting for life to begin and discovering a single, overwhelming purpose. It's about giving your life a purpose.

When even the most fundamental actions are driven by purpose, life seems different. Work becomes a donation. Chores are replaced by care. Relationships become sacred. Growth comes from challenges.

It doesn't matter where you are or what you own; what matters is whether your heart is awake or not.

"Life is never made miserable by circumstances, but only by lack of meaning and purpose," Viktor Frankl told us in Man's Search for Meaning.

I therefore ask that you pause as you end this chapter. Inhale deeply once. "What is one tiny way I can live with meaning today?" is a question to ask oneself.

Go ahead and do it. That one deed could mark the start of a new life as well as a new day.

Key Insights

- Purpose is your compass — guiding both small choices and big decisions.
- Routines can be transformed into rituals of meaning.
- The gap between existing and truly living is purpose.

- Burnout isn't the end — it's a signal to realign.
- Purpose is not discovered once; it is practiced daily.

Your Turn: Sealing Your Purpose

Before you close this book and step back into your daily life, take a moment to pause.

Purpose is not something you only read about; it is something you live.

And living begins with reflection.

Use the space below to write down your thoughts. There are no right or wrong answers. This is your compass, your guide, your truth.

1. Looking Back:

What are the three most powerful insights you are taking away from this book? Why do they matter to you?

____

2. Your Compass:

If you had to describe your purpose in one or two sentences today, what would it be?

____

3. Daily Anchors:

What small daily practices (gratitude, reflection, intentional planning, service, etc.) will you commit to, starting now, to keep yourself aligned with that purpose?

____

4. Integration:

How will you bring purpose into your relationships, your work, your finances, and your personal growth? Write down one specific step for each.

---

5. Legacy:

Imagine yourself many years from now, looking back at your life. What do you hope people will remember about you? What story do you want your life to tell?

Take your time. Write slowly, honestly, and with courage. These answers do not need to be perfect; they only need to be true to you in this moment. As your life evolves, you can return to these pages, reflect again, and refine your compass.

Purpose is not fixed; it grows as you grow. But today, with clarity and intention, you have taken a step toward living your own purposeful life.

Your Daily Compass - One-Line Mantra

Sometimes the simplest words carry the deepest power. While your purpose may be vast and multi-layered, you can distill its essence into a single guiding sentence—a mantra you can return to each day.

This mantra will act as your Daily Compass, reminding you of what matters most, especially in moments of confusion, stress, or distraction.

How to Create Your Mantra:

1. Keep it short – one line only.
2. Make it personal – it should resonate with YOU, not sound like a generic quote.
3. Make it active – phrase it in a way that calls you to live it.
4. Make it inspiring – it should lift you, center you, or strengthen you when you repeat it.

Examples (only as inspiration, not to copy):

- "I live each day to grow, give, and love."
- "My purpose is to serve with courage and compassion."
- "I create meaning through kindness and integrity."
- "I rise, I learn, I contribute."

Your Turn:

Take a quiet moment. Breathe. Reflect on all you've learned, written, and felt while reading this book. Then, write down your one-line mantra below:

My Daily Purpose Mantra:

____

Chapter 4

The Relationship Between Purpose and Money: Prosperity with Values

Part 1: Money as a Servant, Not a Master
The Philosophy Behind Money

We live in a world where every moment seems to have a price tag: the coffee that wakes us up, the phone that connects us, even the peace we seek on weekends. In the 21st century, money has quietly become the language of existence. Money is one of the most powerful forces shaping human civilization. It is more than just paper, coins, or numbers on a screen; it is an instrument that channels human effort, creativity, and resources into tangible impact. With it, schools are built, scientific discoveries are funded, businesses are fueled, and entire communities are lifted from poverty. Hospitals, space exploration, technological revolutions, and even social movements have been made possible because of financial resources.

Money, in its purest form, is energy, a neutral medium of exchange that allows societies to function, grow, and evolve.

Yet, this very tool that can heal and build has also been a double-edged sword.

History is full of conflicts, wars, exploitation, corruption, and personal suffering fueled by the misuse or obsession with money. Families have been torn apart, friendships have been broken, and nations have collapsed because money shifted from being a servant to becoming the master.

Thus, the problem is not money itself, but our relationship with it.

- When money dictates our decisions
- When career choices are driven only by financial gain
- When relationships are measured in material worth
- When personal value is equated with wealth

We fall into a trap. We enslave ourselves to endless pursuit, losing freedom, joy, and meaning. This is when money becomes a silent ruler, chaining us to stress, greed, and dissatisfaction.

But when money is kept in its rightful role as a servant, it unlocks its higher purpose.

It becomes a means to fuel dreams, create opportunities, and bring comfort not just to ourselves but to others. A teacher can use money to educate children, a doctor to save lives, an entrepreneur to create jobs, and a philanthropist to uplift entire communities. In this sense, money transforms into an instrument of empowerment, purpose, and service.

The world's greatest thinkers, philosophers, and leaders have echoed this wisdom for centuries. They remind us that wealth should be used but never worshipped. Mahatma Gandhi captured this truth powerfully when he said,

"The world has enough for everyone's need, but not enough for everyone's greed."

This timeless statement points to the core of a purposeful relationship with money: use it wisely, let it serve humanity, and never let it enslave your spirit.

True prosperity lies not in hoarding wealth but in directing it toward meaningful causes. When we align money with human values—compassion, growth, justice, and creativity—it becomes a force that uplifts rather than divides. In this philosophy, money is not the end goal but the fuel for a deeper purpose, a tool that allows individuals and societies to flourish while preserving dignity and balance.

The Trap of Money as a Master

Do you remember where we started this book? The story of Shashi, a friend of mine who was earning in seven digits but struggling to be a happy and joyful person in life, feeling caught in the "golden cage." He was earning more than he ever imagined, but the work felt empty. Despite luxury lifestyles, he struggled with stress, loneliness, and burnout. His life reveals the truth:

Money cannot buy meaning.

When money controls us, life often turns into an endless chase. People work jobs they despise, sacrifice health and relationships, and live in constant anxiety about having more, yet no amount ever feels enough. This mindset stems from seeing money as the ultimate goal, rather than as a resource to enable a greater purpose.

Money as a Servant: A Tool for Purpose

When money is seen as a servant, it takes on a supportive role. It becomes a tool that enables dreams, fuels passions, and amplifies impact.

The person remains in control of their choices, guided by purpose, not paycheck.

For example,

- Dr. A.P.J. Abdul Kalam, India's "Missile Man" and beloved President, lived a life of remarkable simplicity despite his stature. He earned respect worldwide, yet he did not accumulate wealth for luxury. Instead, he directed his resources toward education, science, and inspiring youth. For him, money was a tool to empower future generations, not a symbol of status.
- Warren Buffett, American business magnate, intelligent investor, and philanthropist, offers another striking example. One of the richest men in the world, Buffett, still lives in the same modest home he bought in 1958. His wealth does not define his happiness; rather, he sees it as a responsibility to give back. Through the Giving Pledge, which he co-founded with Bill and Melinda Gates, Buffett committed to donating over 99% of his fortune to philanthropic causes. Here, money serves humanity instead of enslaving its possessor.

Simplicity as Strength

A purposeful relationship with money often reveals itself in simplicity. Simplicity does not mean poverty; rather, it reflects clarity. When people know their purpose, they do not feel the urge to overspend or hoard wealth. They can enjoy comfort without being trapped by materialism.

Take Ratan Tata, one of India's most respected industrialists. Though he led the massive Tata Group and created global businesses, he is admired for his humility and integrity.

He directed corporate profits toward social development, education, healthcare, and rural upliftment through the Tata Trusts. For him, money was never the end. It was a means to uplift society. Stories of him quietly helping individuals—funding surgeries, supporting startups, or rescuing employees during crises—show how deeply he believed that wealth must serve others.

Money and Inner Freedom

True wealth is not measured by bank accounts but by freedom—the ability to live aligned with one's values. When money is treated as a servant, it liberates us; when treated as a master, it chains us.

Consider Oprah Winfrey. Born into poverty, she rose to become one of the most influential women in the world. Her empire brought her immense wealth, but she repeatedly emphasizes that money is not her master. She invests heavily in causes close to her heart, particularly education for underprivileged girls in Africa through the Oprah Winfrey Leadership Academy.

For her, money is not about flaunting power, but about creating opportunities where none existed.

In India, Infosys co-founder Narayana Murthy embodies this principle.

When he and his team built Infosys, they lived frugally, reinvested every rupee back into the company, and built a culture of fairness. Even after achieving global success, Murthy and his wife, Sudha Murthy, remained committed to philanthropy, particularly in healthcare, libraries, and rural education. Money never dictated their values—it served them.

Reframing Our Relationship with Money

The key is to constantly ask:

Do I own my money, or does money own me?

If every decision is dictated by financial gain, then money has become the master. But if financial resources are directed toward what truly matters- family, growth, service, and impact, then money is in its rightful role.

This reframing has practical benefits.

When people see money as a servant:

- **Stress reduces:** Finances stop being a source of fear and become a source of empowerment.
- **Choices expand:** We can say no to toxic work and yes to opportunities aligned with purpose.
- **Impact multiplies:** Wealth is directed toward causes that uplift communities, not just personal consumption.

The Everyday Hero

It's not only billionaires or leaders who demonstrate this principle.

- Consider a schoolteacher who dedicates part of her salary to sponsor a student's education.
- Or a family that saves money not for lavish vacations, but to care for aging parents.

These acts may not make headlines, but they show the essence of money as a servant: it becomes a tool for love, service, and dignity.

To Sum Up Part 1

Money is not inherently good or bad. It is neutral energy; its power comes from how we use it. When enslaved to greed, it becomes destructive. When guided by purpose, it becomes transformative.

As the Dalai Lama once said, "Wealth should serve humanity, not the other way around."

This is the first step in aligning purpose and money: reclaiming mastery over our financial resources and ensuring they serve our higher values.

Part 2: How Financial Goals Feel Different When Aligned with Deeper Meaning

The Difference Between Earning and Earning with Purpose

Financial goals are part of everyone's life - saving for a house, funding children's education, investing for retirement, or building wealth. But these goals feel profoundly different when they are rooted in purpose rather than comparison, fear, or societal pressure.

Earning with purpose isn't about rejecting money, it's about giving money a mission. It turns numbers into narratives. A savings account isn't just a balance; it's a fund for freedom, growth, or impact. Investments aren't just about returns; they're about fueling dreams, securing loved ones' futures, and enabling contributions to society.

When aligned with deeper meaning, financial goals stop feeling like burdens and start feeling like opportunities. Every rupee or dollar saved, spent, or donated becomes an expression of who you are and what you value.

The Pitfall of Empty Financial Goals

Many people set financial targets without asking why.

For instance, "I want to earn 10 crore by the age of 40" or "I want a million dollars in the bank." These goals may provide temporary motivation but often lack emotional connection.

Without purpose, people achieve such goals yet feel strangely unfulfilled.

Studies on random lottery winners reveal this paradox clearly: sudden wealth does not automatically bring happiness. In fact, many winners report higher stress, strained relationships, and loss of meaning after acquiring vast sums of money. Why? Because money alone cannot anchor life, it must be tied to values, contribution, and purpose.

Financial Goals Aligned with Values

When money serves a purpose beyond self, it creates energy rather than emptiness.

Let's explore how meaningful financial goals play out in different contexts:

1. **For Families:** Saving isn't just about accumulation; it's about building security, ensuring quality education, and creating experiences together. Parents who view money as a tool for providing stability and opportunities feel more fulfilled, even with modest incomes.
2. **For Entrepreneurs:** Profit becomes more than personal wealth. It fuels innovation, creates jobs, and supports causes. Entrepreneurs who tie their ventures to purpose, be it sustainability, empowerment, or inclusion, often feel deeper satisfaction than those chasing valuations alone.

3. **For Professionals:** Aligning career income with purpose means choosing workplaces that respect values, offer growth, and allow for impact. A smaller paycheck in a fulfilling role can bring greater joy than a large paycheck in a toxic environment.

Bill Gates: Redefining Wealth Through Purpose

Through Microsoft, Bill Gates amassed one of the greatest fortunes in history. However, his life's course was altered when he started to consider a more profound question:

"What good is prosperity if it doesn't help lives?"

Gates committed himself to the Bill & Melinda Gates Foundation, which aims to eradicate disease, enhance education, and guarantee equal opportunity globally, after leaving day-to-day operations.

His goal shifted from creating computer software to creating human solutions.

He now bases every financial choice he makes on that goal, from support for vaccines to climate innovation. He demonstrates that financial capital may become social capital when driven by purpose by reinvesting riches into effect rather than allowing money to grow.

A timeless lesson can be learned from Gates's journey: profit follows significance when purpose leads. In this sense, wealth becomes a measure of what we facilitate rather than what we own.

Mr. Azim Premji: Beyond Business

One of the most renowned philanthropists in India is Mr. Azim Premji, a former chairman of Wipro. Even though Wipro helped him amass enormous riches, his financial objectives went beyond company expansion.

Driven by a sense of purpose, he donated the majority of his wealth, more than $21 billion, to the Azim Premji Foundation, which prioritizes social development and education.

For him, having money is a way to change millions of people's lives, not just a way to achieve personal achievement.

Premji's narrative serves as an example of how financial objectives that are in line with greater meaning produce legacies rather than just wealth.

The Psychology of Purpose-Driven Money

Researchers in positive psychology emphasize that people derive greater satisfaction from "self-transcendent goals, those that extend beyond the self, than from self-focused ones. When money is linked to contribution, community, or legacy, it brings longer-lasting fulfillment.

For instance, Harvard's Study of Adult Development, one of the longest studies on happiness, shows that wealth does not predict long-term happiness as strongly as meaningful relationships and purpose. However, when money is directed toward nurturing relationships, family support, community, and experiences, it amplifies happiness.

Reframing Success

When financial goals are guided by meaning, success is measured differently:

- Instead of "How much did I earn?", the question becomes, "What impact did my earnings create?"
- Instead of "How many assets do I own?", the focus shifts to "How have my assets supported my values and the lives of others?"
- Instead of "Am I rich?", it becomes, "Am I fulfilled, free, and impactful?"

This reframing transforms how we chase, use, and experience money.

Sudha Murthy: Reframing the Lens

Sudha Murthy, author and philanthropist, has consistently highlighted the difference between money for status and money for purpose.

While she and Narayana Murthy built enormous wealth through Infosys, Sudha has dedicated much of her life to philanthropy through the Infosys Foundation.

Her financial goals revolve around social development, women's empowerment, and healthcare. She often says,

"Money is not important. What you do with it is important."

Her approach reminds us that money aligned with values magnifies meaning.

The Spiritual Dimension

Many spiritual traditions echo the idea that money tied to meaning transcends materialism.

- **In Hindu philosophy,** *Artha* (wealth) is considered one of the four key aims of life, but it is never to be pursued in isolation. It must be balanced with Dharma (righteousness).

- **Similarly, Buddhism emphasizes right livelihood,** earning wealth in ways that support compassion and integrity.

This perspective highlights that financial goals divorced from purpose are incomplete. True prosperity lies in harmony between wealth and values.

Financial Goals with a Human Face

- A young professional deciding to live modestly so he can fund his sibling's college education.
- A couple saving not for a bigger house, but to adopt a child and provide a nurturing home.
- A small business owner who reinvests profits into creating local jobs rather than maximizing personal luxuries.

These stories, though less visible than billionaires' philanthropy, show that anyone can align money with purpose.

How to Align Your Own Financial Goals

1. **Ask "Why?" Behind Every Goal**

   If your goal is to earn more, ask yourself: why? Is it for security, freedom, family, impact, or prestige? This clarifies whether your goals are purpose-driven or ego-driven.

2. **Define Your Core Values**

   Write down your top 3–5 values (e.g., family, service, growth, freedom). Align financial decisions with these.

3. **Reframe Budgets as Value-Based**

   Instead of seeing budgets as restrictions, view them as value statements. Every expense reflects what you prioritize.

4. **Integrate Giving Early**

   You don't need to be rich to give. Even small amounts directed toward causes close to your heart make money more meaningful.

5. **Balance Now and Later**

   Purpose-driven financial goals honor both present joy and future security. It's not just about hoarding for tomorrow but living meaningfully today.

Key Insights

Financial goals are not just numbers; they are reflections of our values. When aligned with deeper meaning, money becomes not just a currency of exchange but a currency of purpose.

As Maya Angelou beautifully put it, "I have found that among its other benefits, giving liberates the soul of the giver."

Part 3: Defining Your "Money Story" and Aligning It with Purpose

Practical Exercises

Exercise 1: Discovering Your Money Story

Your money story is like the "operating system" running silently in your life. It influences how you negotiate salaries, how you spend at the grocery store, how you give (or don't give), and how secure or anxious you feel about the future.

Steps to Do This:

1. **Recall Childhood Memories:** Write about your earliest memory of money.
   - Did your parents argue about it?
   - Did you see money as joy (gifts, festivals, celebrations) or as stress (debts, scarcity)?
2. **Identify Inherited Beliefs:** List phrases you heard growing up.
   - "We can't afford it."
   - "Money is evil."

- "Save every rupee."
- "Money makes you free."

3. **Notice Emotional Patterns Today:** How do you feel about paying bills? About receiving a bonus? Do you avoid checking your bank balance?
4. **Map Behavior:** Track if you overspend, hoard, under-invest, or give generously.

Case Example:

- ➢ Oprah Winfrey grew up in poverty but redefined her money story by seeing wealth as a tool for empowerment. She often says, "The greatest gift you can give yourself is a life of purpose."
- ➢ On the other hand, Warren Buffett grew up during the Great Depression.

His story taught him frugality, which he carried even after becoming a billionaire (still living in the same Omaha house).

Remember: Your money story is not fixed; you can rewrite it, just as they did.

Exercise 2: Redefining Money as a Servant

Money becomes destructive when it controls your choices. But when you see it as a servant, it becomes fuel for what matters most.

Steps to Do This:

1. **Draw a T-chart with two columns.**
    - **Left column:** "When money controls me…" (E.g., I stay in a job I hate only for the salary, I buy gadgets to impress friends, I feel constant stress about keeping up with others).

- **Right column:** "When I control money…" (E.g., I use money to take my parents on pilgrimage, I pay for health check-ups, I save to launch my startup).

2. **Write at least 5 examples per column.**
3. **Circle the right-column examples and ask: What habits will help me do more of these?**

Case Example:

➢ **Azim Premji (India):** Known for his frugality despite being a billionaire. Instead of being controlled by wealth, he donated most of his fortune to education initiatives, making money serve millions of children.

➢ **JK Rowling:** After gaining massive wealth from Harry Potter, she refused to let it dominate her life. She said, "I will not be defined by money but by the impact of my stories."

Remember: This exercise flips the script; you no longer work for money; money works for your purpose.

Exercise 3: Aligning Financial Goals with Purpose

Without purpose, financial goals can feel hollow. Purpose gives them soul.

Steps to Do This:

1. List your top 3 life values (family, creativity, freedom, service, health, spirituality).
2. Under each, write how money can support that value.
3. Convert it into a SMART goal (Specific, Measurable, Achievable, Relevant, Time-bound).

Example:

Value	How Money Supports	SMART Goal
Family	Secure kids' education	Save ₹20 lakhs in 10 years in an education fund
Creativity	Invest in filmmaking passion	Allocate ₹5,000/month to creative projects
Service	Support rural healthcare	Donate ₹1 lakh annually to NGOs

Case Example:

- **Ratan Tata:** His financial goal was not just profit but nation-building. He aligned corporate profits with values like dignity, the nation's growth, and ethics.
- **Elon Musk:** Though criticized, his financial goals align with his purpose—making humanity multi-planetary.

Remember: When money goals are tied to values, every rupee or dollar feels more meaningful.

Final & Important: Practical Action Plan

Dreams collapse without structure. This turns reflection into results.

Steps to Do This:

1. **Track Spending for 30 Days:** Use expense tracking apps on your phone or a simple notebook.
2. **Categorize:** Highlight which expenses serve a purpose (health, learning, giving) and which don't (status spending, impulsive buys).
3. **Reallocate:** Even 10% shifted from wasteful to purposeful categories creates massive change.

4. **Automate:** Automate savings, investments, and donations so discipline doesn't rely only on your willpower.
5. **Review:** Every 6 months, revisit your purpose-aligned financial plan.

Case Example:

- A Pune couple realized they spent ₹5,000/month on dining out. By reallocating half of it toward their daughter's robotics classes, they aligned money with education values.

Remember: Action builds momentum. Small but consistent shifts redefine your financial destiny.

Bringing It All Together

Money is one of humanity's most powerful tools. It can heal or harm, liberate or enslave, inspire generosity or deepen greed. The key is how we use it. Through this chapter, we've explored how purpose transforms money from a stressful pursuit into a meaningful companion.

When money is aligned with your values:

- It ceases to be a despot
- It becomes a servant.
- It starts amplifying your vision instead of controlling it.

From billionaires like Warren Buffett, Ratan Tata, Azim Premji, Bill & Melinda Gates to everyday families making conscious choices, the lesson is the same: Purpose gives money soul.

To Sum it Up

Think of money as energy, neutral in itself. Just as electricity can light a home or burn it down, money can serve love or fear, ego or compassion. Purpose is the switch that determines which path it takes.

When you look at your bank account, don't just ask:

- "How much is there?"

Ask instead:

- "What story is this money telling about my values?"
- "Who is benefitting from how I spend, save, and give?"

This shift from accumulation to alignment will change not only your financial destiny but also the lives of those around you.

Money magnifies who you already are. If you are fearful, it will magnify fear. If you are generous, it will magnify generosity. The invitation of this chapter is to let purpose be your compass so that money - whether little or large- becomes a tool of creation, service, and joy.

As Mahatma Gandhi said: "The world has enough for everyone's need, but not enough for everyone's greed." May your money journey reflect not greed, but purpose.

Chapter 5

Purpose and Health: Powering Your Life's Meaning

Priya the Perseverant Health Enthusiast

Let me introduce you to Priya, the most sensible girl in our class, who is now a teacher.

Priya wants to be a loving mother to her two children and support her students in having big dreams.

However, she felt stuck last year. She was worn out and anxious from long school days, never-ending grading, and managing a home.

She remained up late, skipped meals, and lacked the enthusiasm to motivate her students or play with her children. Priya realized she needed a change after losing her temper with a student one day.

She only wanted to feel alive again for her children and her classroom, not for a flawless physique.

Priya began modestly, going to bed by 10 p.m. to get enough sleep, taking quick walks after supper to move her body, and practicing deep breathing for ten minutes every morning to help her relax. These were straightforward methods to further her goals rather than elaborate solutions.

She soon felt more alert, grinned more with her children, and infused her instruction with fresh vitality.

Priya's experience demonstrates that being healthy isn't about looking attractive; rather, it's about having the fortitude to pursue your goals, regardless of your identity.

This chapter examines how your body, mind, and heart work together, how being well gives you the motivation to achieve your objectives, and how simple habits like rest, exercise, and mindfulness may help you live your best life. To illustrate how health drives purpose, we'll look at the same well-known figures, Oprah Winfrey, A.R. Rahman, and Serena Williams, who were mentioned in the last chapter. We'll wrap up with easy steps you can take.

Health: The Energy for Your Purpose

What motivates you, the reason you wake up every day, is your purpose. It could be raising a family, teaching children, creating music, or lending a hand to others. But you need strength, energy, and attention to pursue your objective. Herein lies the role of health. Health is about empowering you to do what matters most, not about looking like a movie star. A peaceful heart helps you deal with difficult days, a strong body helps you persevere, and a clear mind lets you think clearly.

Ignoring your health could lead to burnout or giving up.

However, you may accomplish more for your mission if you take care of yourself.

Consider this: a parent requires patience to guide their children, a teacher needs energy to lead a class, and a musician needs focus to create. Health keeps you going toward your objective, much like fuel in a motor. You're not being self-centered when you eat healthily, exercise, and get enough sleep; rather, you're ensuring that you can attend events that you enjoy.

Let's use real-world examples to comprehend it.

Oprah Winfrey

TV personality and many people's helper, Oprah Winfrey, strives to uplift people via her programs and charitable endeavors. She operates a business, hosts events, and supports children's schools, all of which need a lot of energy.

Oprah has discussed her health issues, such as overindulging in junk food and experiencing stress.

- She now writes in a notebook to decompress
- Walks or practices yoga to maintain her strength
- And consults a therapist to feel at ease

These behaviors enable her to continue to inspire millions of people, not just make her seem good. Oprah demonstrates how you can make a difference in the world by taking care of yourself.

A.R. Rahman

The goal of renowned Indian musician A.R. Rahman, who won an Oscar for Slumdog Millionaire, is to make heartfelt music. It takes a lot of energy to write songs, record late at night, and perform.

Rahman maintains his health with easy routines:

- He spends time with his family to feel joyful
- practices yoga to keep his body supple
- and meditates to stay focused

These decisions enable him to continue creating lovely music, demonstrating how a creative goal can be supported by health.

> **Serena Williams**
>
> One of the greatest tennis players of all time, Serena Williams, aspires to win matches and encourage women, particularly Black women, to have big dreams.
>
> She requires a strong heart to withstand pressure, a sharp intellect for planning, and an incredibly powerful physique for matches.
>
> Serena relies on her family for affection, exercises hard with weights and running, and employs mental tactics like visualizing her victories.
>
> Her good health practices enable her to continue winning and inspiring others, demonstrating that having good health is essential for achieving large goals.

These famous people show that health gives you the power to live your purpose, whether it's inspiring, creating, or winning.

How Your Mind, Body, and Heart Work Together

Health is a combination of your body (your physical state), mind (your mental state), and heart (your emotional state). Like puzzle pieces, these three components are interconnected. You have a reason to care for each of them since your purpose is what keeps them all together.

- **Mind:** You can think clearly, solve issues, and maintain concentration when your mind is in good condition. Making wise decisions and staying true to your goals might be challenging when you're anxious or exhausted.
- **Body:** Whether you're running, teaching, or creating, having a strong body gives you the energy to execute your job. It's difficult to continue when you're ill or weak.

- **Heart:** You can connect with people, overcome adversity, and maintain hope when your heart is at ease. It's more difficult to pursue your goals when you're depressed or irritated.

The others suffer when one section does. For instance, you might not sleep well (body) and feel grumpy (heart) if you're anxious (thinking). However, you feel happier (heart) and think more clearly (mind) if you exercise (body). In order to be your best self, your purpose compels you to take care of all three.

Practices: Mindfulness, Exercise, and Rest to Support Your Purpose

Maintaining your health is a method to support your purpose, not a chore. Simple routines like rest, exercise, and mindfulness offer you the power, energy, and focus you need to do the things that really matter. Let's examine each one, its benefits, and the ways in which our well-known individuals employ them.

1. Mindfulness: Clearing Your Mind

Being mindful entails focusing on the present moment, whether it is through writing, meditation, or silent thought. It keeps you composed, improves your ability to concentrate, and helps you manage stress so you can stay focused on your goals.

Why It Helps: Being mindful helps you stay connected to your mission, sharpen your mind, and lessen anxiety. It's similar to clearing your head so you can see clearly.

For instance, Oprah Winfrey

Oprah needs to have a clean head in order to fulfill her mission of inspiring. She keeps a daily journal and practices meditation to maintain her focus. These practices demonstrate how mindfulness drives purpose by assisting her in making wise decisions and adhering to her objectives.

How to Do It: Spend 10 minutes a day on mindfulness. Try a free meditation app (like Insight Timer), write about what you're grateful for, or sit quietly and think about your purpose. Even a short pause can help you feel centered.

2. Exercise: Moving Your Body

Walking, dancing, or stretching are examples of physical activity. It gives you more energy to accomplish your goals by making you happier, more powerful, and more alert.

Why It Helps: Exercise improves your mood, provides you with energy, and sharpens your mind. It's similar to recharging your body's batteries.

For instance, Serena Williams

Serena requires a very powerful body to fulfill her mission of inspiring and winning. To stay prepared for tennis, she stretches, runs, and lifts weights. Her ability to play and inspire others is a result of these behaviors, demonstrating how exercise promotes meaning.

How to Do It: Five days a week, move your body for twenty to thirty minutes. Try doing something you enjoy, like yoga, dancing, or walking. You can feel prepared for your mission with even a quick stroll.

3. Rest: Recharging Your Energy

Rest entails getting a good night's sleep or spending time to unwind. It keeps your heart healthy, your body healing, and your mind functioning properly so you can continue.

Why It Helps: Beneficial Rest prevents burnout, improves memory, and calms emotions. For your purpose, it's similar to pressing the reset button.

For instance, A.R. Rahman

Rahman needs energy for lengthy studio nights in order to accomplish his goal of creating music. He takes quick breaks to unwind and makes sure to get a good night's sleep. These routines enable him to continue being creative and producing music, demonstrating how purpose is supported by rest.

How to Do It: Try to get between seven and nine hours every night. Try establishing a sleep ritual, such as putting your phone away for half an hour before bed. Every day, take five to ten minutes to relax your thoughts by closing your eyes or taking deep breaths.

How to Make These Habits Beneficial to You

These behaviors are most effective when they align with your mission. If you're a teacher, practice meditation to maintain patience, stay active to keep up with students, and take breaks to create engaging lesson plans. If you're a parent, practice mindfulness to spend time with your children, work out to keep up with their energy, and take breaks to maintain composure. You may support what you love in this way.

The Cycle of Purpose and Health

Your health and your purpose are mutually beneficial. When you are aware of your purpose, you want to maintain your health in order to continue. You have more energy to pursue your goals when you're well. It resembles a circle that intensifies over time.

Our well-known individuals demonstrate this:

- **Oprah Winfrey:** She walks, meditates, and converses with friends because she wants to inspire others. These activities give her the vitality she needs to lead.
- **A.R. Rahman:** His goal of creating music motivates him to practice yoga and relax, which enables him to write more tunes.
- **Serena Williams:** She trains hard because she wants to win, which keeps her strong for tennis and motivates others.

Everyone may benefit from this circle: your purpose drives you to take care of your health, and your health enables you to fulfill your purpose.

Challenges and Simple Hacks

Sometimes, it's hard to focus on health. Here are common problems and easy ways to fix them:

- **No Time:** Life is busy, but you can do small things. Try a 5-minute meditation or walking during lunch. Oprah fits quick walks into her packed days.
- **No Money:** Health doesn't need cash. Walk for free, use YouTube for yoga, or eat simple, healthy foods like rice and veggies. Rahman uses affordable yoga to stay fit.
- **Feeling Lazy:** Some days, you don't want to try. Think of health as helping your purpose, not a chore. Serena sees exercise as part of winning, not a burden.
- **No Resources:** If you don't have a gym or healthy food nearby, use what you have—like walking or stretching at home. Rahman uses simple habits anyone can try.

These fixes show that anyone can make health work for their purpose, no matter where they are.

To Sum It Up

Health is more than simply a method to look nice; it's like the battery that powers your purpose. Your mission offers you a reason to take care of your body, mind, and heart, all of which work together to keep you strong. As Priya did for her teaching and children, you can support what you love by adopting simple habits like mindfulness, exercise, and rest. Celebrities like Serena Williams, A.R. Rahman, and Oprah Winfrey demonstrate how their health enables them to succeed, inspire, and create. You are stronger for your mission when you take care of your health, and your purpose motivates you to maintain your health. To begin this cycle in your life, try the methods listed below.

Exercises

Here are easy steps to try for 30 days to connect health with your purpose:

1. Find Your Purpose (15 minutes)

Write one sentence about what drives you (like "I want to teach kids to love learning"). Think about how health helps you do this. Read it every day.

2. Mindfulness (10 minutes daily)

Try a 10-minute meditation (use a free app like Insight Timer) or write about something you're thankful for. Ask, "How can I live my purpose today?"

3. Exercise (20-30 minutes, 5 days a week)

Move your body with something fun, like walking or dancing, for 150 minutes a week. Notice how it gives you energy for your purpose.

4. Rest (Daily)

Get 7-9 hours of sleep with a bedtime routine (no phone before bed). Take a 5-minute break each day to relax, like breathing deeply.

5. Weekly Check-In (30 minutes)

Every Sunday, write about your week: How did these habits help your purpose? What was hard? Make small changes if needed.

6. Connect with Others (1 hour weekly)

Talk to a friend or family member who supports your purpose. Share your goals or do something together to feel strong.

Chapter 6

Purpose and Career Discovering Your True Calling

One of the most significant factors influencing people's lives is their work. A large portion of our daily routine, sense of accomplishment, and even identity is linked to our employment from the moment we enter adulthood. While some people drag themselves to the office feeling disinterested and uninspired, others wake up invigorated by the notion of their tasks. What is the reason behind this disparity?

Purpose holds the key to the solution.

Work becomes more than just a source of income when it is in line with a purpose; it becomes a source of enthusiasm, vitality, and even heritage. In-depth discussions of the distinctions between a job, a career, and a calling will be covered in this chapter, along with how purpose transforms work into passion, real-life examples of professionals who changed their careers, and a potent exercise that will help you match your personal values with your work.

Consider this chapter as a manual rather than a brief essay because it is purposefully lengthy and informative. Examples, studies, and useful observations are included to help you take a moment to ponder carefully on your own career path.

Section 1: Difference Between a Job, a Career, and a Calling

Let's start with the foundation: what do we mean by job, career, and calling? These three words are often used interchangeably, but they actually represent very different ways of relating to work.

A Job: The Survival Mode

A job is work we do mostly to make money. The motivation is simple: to survive, pay bills, and put food on the table. Jobs are frequently transactional in nature, requiring you to trade money for your time and effort. Jobs may not always feel significant, even though they can be honest and essential.

Example: In Delhi, Ravi is employed as a cashier at a supermarket. Among his responsibilities are welcoming clients, processing payments, and scanning goods. Although he doesn't detest his work, he also doesn't feel enthusiastic about it. He views it as a means of providing for his family. That's what a job is all about: it provides for urgent cash necessities.

A Career: The Growth Path

A career is more than just a means of subsistence. It's about reaching milestones, gaining recognition, and developing knowledge. Long-term dedication, training, and status are all necessary for careers. Career success is determined by accomplishments, titles, and promotions.

Example: Annie practices law in New York. She began her career as an intern, advanced to associate, and is currently a senior partner in her company. She has dedicated years to her studies and work, and being a lawyer is deeply ingrained in her identity. For her, work is more than simply a source of income; it's an opportunity to develop and prove herself.

A Calling: The Fulfillment Path

The most profound level of involvement with work is a calling. At this point, it seems impossible to separate who you are from what you do. Even if the labor isn't always simple, it always seems worthwhile. Individuals who pursue a calling frequently say that they would continue to conduct their work even in the absence of compensation.

Example (Africa): Maya works as a physician in a small Kenyan community. She knows her work saves lives and has an impact on her community, so even with minimal resources and hard hours, she feels incredibly fulfilled. She views medicine as her life's purpose rather than just a career.

Everyday Comparisons

- A delivery driver may treat his work as a job, or he may see it as a calling if he believes he is providing essential services that help people live comfortably.
- A teacher might treat teaching as a career, focusing on promotions and recognition, or as a calling if she believes her real purpose is to shape young minds.

Key Insight: Jobs pay the bills, careers build growth, and callings bring meaning. None is "better" than the others, but knowing where you stand helps you make conscious decisions about where you want to go.

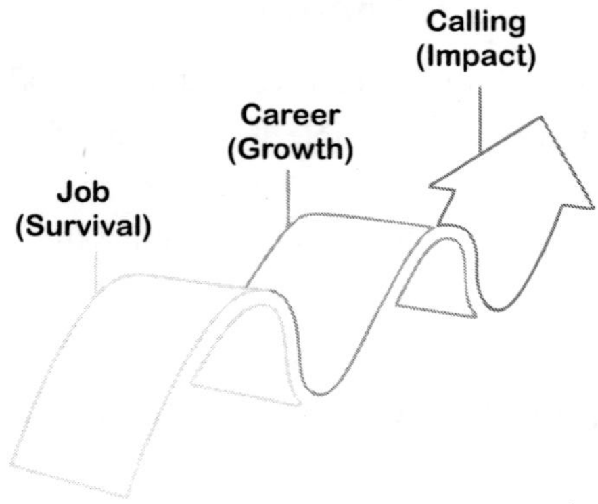

Section 2: How Purpose Can Turn Work Into Passion

Many people think that passion is something you find by accident, similar to magic. In actuality, discovering a purpose in your work frequently leads to passion. The "why" underlying the "what" is provided by purpose. Daily routines that would otherwise appear robotic are given context and significance.

Purpose as the Engine of Passion

Consider purpose like an automobile's engine. No matter how well-maintained the car appears on the outside, it cannot move without it. The underlying motivation that drives our behavior is called purpose. It explains why we get up and decide to work on things that could seem routine or repetitious.

For Instance:

- **Without purpose:** A waiter may consider his work to be monotonous and exhausting, consisting solely of moving plates.
- **With purpose:** The same server can see himself as contributing to happy moments made by couples and families. All of a sudden,

working long hours feels more fulfilling since he is making a positive impact on something greater than himself.

The Why Behind the What

This is what it means when we say purpose provides the "why" behind the "what." What is the action: answering emails, teaching a class, making deliveries, or writing reports. The why is the deeper reason — helping others, sharing knowledge, ensuring people get what they need, or contributing to a greater goal. When people forget the why, work feels mechanical, like running on autopilot. But when they rediscover it, even ordinary routines take on meaning.

- **Purpose in Action**

  Imagine that two nurses are employed at the same hospital. They both deal with stressful situations and lengthy hours. One feels worn out and bitter because one perceives the effort as never-ending. Reminding herself that each patient she assists is someone's parent, kid, or friend inspires the other. The distinction? Purpose.

- **How Purpose Changes Perspective**

  You stop viewing work as merely a list of tasks when you connect it to a higher meaning. A customer service representative, for instance, can feel exhausted from fielding calls all the time. However, the same calls feel more significant if she reframes her role as "making someone's hectic day easier." Although obstacles still exist, this change in viewpoint fosters resilience and motivation.

- **Passion Grows from Purpose**

  Purpose is like fuel. When you connect your role to something important, even mundane tasks become more fascinating.

A Chinese factory worker is more content with his job if he believes he is contributing to the feeding of families throughout the world than if he sees it as boring and useless. Purpose transforms drudgery into devotion. Eventually, this sense of purpose turns into a genuine excitement for the work.

- **Research Insight**

According to psychological research, those who find meaning in their work report greater resilience, job happiness, and even better physical health. According to neuroscience, doing meaningful work increases our motivation and engagement by activating reward pathways in the brain. In other words, your brain rewards you for accomplishing something that aligns with your ideals.

- **From Ikigai:**

In Japan, there is the concept of ikigai: "a reason for being."

People who identify their ikigai, the sweet spot where passion, mission, vocation, and profession meet, often live longer and healthier lives. This cultural philosophy demonstrates how purpose sustains passion across decades.

- **Everyday Examples**

Think of a teacher. Without purpose, teaching may feel like endless grading and classroom management. With purpose, it becomes about shaping the next generation, sparking curiosity, and building futures. The tasks remain the same, but the meaning makes all the difference.

Key Insight:

Purpose doesn't always mean changing jobs. Often, it's about changing how you view the job you already have. By aligning your tasks with your values, you unlock a deeper motivation that naturally turns into passion.

Section 3: Real-Life Stories of Career Realignment with Purpose

The Teacher Who Revolutionized Learning with QR-Enabled Textbooks (India)

Meet Ranjitsinh Disale, a primary school teacher from Solapur, Maharashtra (India). In 2009, he arrived at a government school that was barely functioning, with poor attendance, especially among girls, and little interest from parents. Instead of accepting it, he made it his mission to transform the learning experience of students.

One of his most creative ideas came when he saw QR codes being used in shops for payments through UPI (Unified Payment Interface). He thought: "Why not embed them in textbooks?"

Soon, his students could scan codes to access audio poems, video lessons, and assignments in Marathi. Learning suddenly became exciting and accessible, even for those who couldn't attend school daily. Parents, too, began investing in smartphones to support their children.

The impact was remarkable. Attendance jumped to nearly 100%, girls stayed in school longer, and the approach of parents towards girls' education changed. His idea spread across Maharashtra and later India, with NCERT including QR codes in national textbooks.

In 2020, he won the Global Teacher Prize and shared half of his $1 million award with other finalists.

Fighting Food Waste with Olio (England)

Meet Tessa Clarke and Saasha Celestial-One, co-founders of Olio, an app headquartered in the UK that facilitates the sharing of excess food between businesses and neighbors.

What started off as a tiny experiment in 2015 has developed into a well-known platform that addresses food waste and fosters community.

Both founders had stable corporate jobs but were unfulfilled. They had an idea for a basic app that would allow extra food to be listed and picked up for free because they were fed up with the waste that comes with daily life.

Millions of meals were shared, local ties were strengthened, and the concept gained international attention, including the UN Momentum for Change Award.

Personality Insight: Where Strength Meets Purpose

- **Empathy:** Ranjitsinh connected with students' struggles in rural India, while Tessa and Saasha listened to communities frustrated by waste. In both cases, understanding others' needs fueled meaningful solutions.
- **Creativity:** A QR code became an educational lifeline in one story; in the other, a simple app became a tool for sharing food and reducing waste.
- **Persistence:** From convincing hesitant parents to pushing for national policy, or from pitching a new startup idea to scaling it globally, determination carried these efforts forward.

- **Collaboration and Values:** Whether by earning parents' trust or building neighborhood networks, each aligned their work with deeper values of fairness, sustainability, and social good.

Together, these stories show that when empathy, creativity, and persistence are aligned with a larger purpose, ordinary roles become extraordinary callings, creating passion and lasting impact.

Learning:

These two tales, one from a contemporary English city and the other from a classroom in rural India, demonstrate the same idea: labor becomes passion when it is done with purpose. The idea's ability to match individual strengths with worthwhile objectives is more important than its magnitude. Simple innovations like food-sharing applications or QR codes can have a lasting influence when they are guided by values, empathy, creativity, and perseverance. The takeaway for readers is unmistakable: when your abilities align with a greater purpose, your career becomes a calling.

To Sum it Up

We've explored the three layers of work: jobs, careers, and callings. Jobs help us survive, careers help us grow, and callings help us thrive with meaning. Purpose acts as the bridge between these categories. It turns routine into passion and helps us sustain motivation through challenges. Real-life stories from different parts of the world show that it's possible to pivot, no matter your age or background. The common theme is alignment: when values and work match, fulfillment follows.

Exercises

Identifying Values vs. Job Roles

Now let's turn the insights inward. This exercise is designed to help you reflect on your own work and its connection to your values.

Step 1: List Your Core Values

Write down 5–7 values that matter most to you. Examples: creativity, family, service, freedom, stability, growth, health.

Step 2: Describe Your Current Job Role

Note your daily responsibilities. Be specific. Examples: managing client accounts, coding software, teaching lessons, and handling customer service.

Step 3: Compare Values and Roles

Match your values to your work tasks. Where do they align? Where do they conflict?

- If you value creativity but your work is repetitive, there is a mismatch.
- If you value service and you work in healthcare, there is alignment.

Step 4: Identify Gaps

Ask yourself: Which values are currently unmet in my work?

Step 5: Plan Adjustments

Brainstorm practical steps. Can you reshape your current role to better fit your values? Or is a larger career shift needed?

Your Progress Worksheet

Use this template to make the exercise practical:

My Core Value	Part of My Job That Matches This Value	Part of My Job That Conflicts With This Value	Possible Adjustments
Creativity	Designing presentations	Repetitive reporting tasks	Automate reports, request more creative projects
Service	Helping customers solve issues	Selling products I don't believe in	Move toward service-focused roles
Growth	Learning new tools	Few training opportunities	Ask for a learning budget, take external courses

Fill this table for yourself with your own values and tasks.

Final Thought

Purpose is not a theoretical idea; it is the driving force behind both lives and careers. We can advance in our professions and find stability in our jobs, but we can only find fulfillment in our calling. The good news is that if we align our job with our beliefs, we can find purpose in any role. Keep in mind that doing something that has meaning not only earns a living but also makes life worthwhile.

Chapter 7

Purpose and Relationships

Why Purpose Needs Relationships

It is not in our nature to dwell in solitude. We are surrounded by other people from the time of our birth: parents who raise us, communities that mold us, friends who support us, and partners who go with us. The realization that purpose cannot be fully realized in solitude lies at the core of this interrelated life. Love and support, teaching and learning, giving and receiving, influencing and being influenced, and the space between us are all places where purpose flourishes.

Even though a person may find their calling in the quiet of their own heart, it is only when it affects other people's lives that it takes root and grows. Purpose grows on the soil of relationships. They give us the difficulties that help us grow as well as the sustenance. They are amplifiers that increase the effect of our decisions and mirrors that show who we are becoming.

In this chapter, we explore how purpose strengthens our bonds with those closest to us—our partners, friends, families, and communities. We also look at the ripple effect: how living authentically with purpose inspires others and multiplies impact far beyond what we can see. Together, these insights reveal that purpose is not only about self-discovery but also about co-creation.

The Foundation of Purposeful Relationships

At the core of every meaningful relationship lies a foundation that goes deeper than convenience or surface-level attraction. This foundation is built upon shared values, mutual respect, and an alignment of deeper meaning. Without this grounding, relationships may still exist, but they are often fragile, easily shaken by misunderstandings, external pressures, or the passage of time.

However, relationships take on a new dimension when there is a sense of purpose.

They acquire direction, clarity, and resilience. Even though two friends may laugh and share experiences, their shared values, whether they be honesty, creativity, progress, or compassion, are what keep the connection going when things outside of it change. Even if a family may share a residence, the shared values of the members, whether integrity, service, or education, are what make the home a meaningful entity.

This does not imply that all partners in a relationship need to share the same goals. Instead, it indicates that their objectives and inner ideals are in harmony. Individuality is permitted in purposeful interactions, but a feeling of shared adventure is also fostered. They serve as a reminder that there are two aspects of life: individual fulfillment and group prosperity.

For instance, consider a teacher and a student. The teacher's purpose may be to ignite curiosity, while the student's purpose may be to explore and grow. Though their purposes are different, they complement one another, creating a relationship that nurtures both. Similarly, in a marriage, one partner may be driven by creativity and the other by service, but together, they may build a shared life rooted in mutual respect and a vision of contribution.

When we see relationships through the lens of purpose, we move beyond superficial measures, status, wealth, and convenience, and into the realm of meaning. This shift is what makes bonds last and flourish. Purpose is the invisible thread that holds relationships together when circumstances change, when challenges arise, and when the initial spark fades.

How Purpose Strengthens Love, Friendship, Family, and Community

Purpose is not a private possession. It is a force that strengthens the connections we share with others, giving them depth and durability. Love, friendship, family, and community, four of the most significant arenas of human life, are all enriched when infused with purpose.

Purpose in Love

Romantic love often begins with attraction, excitement, and passion. Yet, history and human experience remind us that these emotions alone are rarely enough to sustain a lifetime partnership. Purpose elevates love from a fleeting feeling to an enduring collaboration.

When two people are aligned in values and vision, their love becomes more than a personal comfort. It becomes a partnership of meaning.

Couples who share a sense of purpose view their relationship not merely as a source of happiness, but as a joint mission, whether it is to raise children with strong values, contribute to their community, or support each other's growth. This shared purpose becomes a reservoir of strength during conflict, illness, or financial strain.

Across cultures, marriage has long been viewed not just as a union of two individuals but as a shared project of life. In India, marriages were traditionally seen as alliances between families that extended beyond personal desires, ensuring cultural continuity and social contribution. In modern contexts, too, couples who see themselves as co-creators of a meaningful life often report deeper satisfaction and resilience.

Purpose transforms love into something greater: a commitment not only to each other but to a larger vision. It changes the question from "How can this relationship make me happy?" to "What can we build together that matters?"

Purpose in Friendship

Friendship is one of life's greatest treasures. True friends are not bound only by shared hobbies or proximity but by shared values and mutual respect.

Purpose makes friendship stronger by turning it into a partnership of growth.

Friendships also serve to spread purpose. Friends frequently challenge and encourage one another in subtle but enduring ways. The partnership between Steve Jobs and Steve Wozniak serves as an example of how friendship and a shared vision can transform entire industries. In daily life, a friend's decision to uphold integrity or discipline frequently changes the peer group's culture.

Purposeful friends hold each other accountable, celebrate authenticity, and challenge one another to live in alignment with their values. They walk alongside us not just during fun times but through adversity, reminding us of who we are and what we stand for.

History offers powerful examples:

- Martin Luther King Jr. and Ralph Abernathy, whose friendship fortified the American civil rights movement

- Rabindranath Tagore and Mahatma Gandhi, whose respect and dialogue strengthened both their missions.

These friendships were not just personal bonds; they were alliances rooted in shared purpose, creating ripples of change far beyond the individuals involved.

In everyday life, too, purposeful friendships can be transformative. A friend who encourages you to pursue your dreams, live with integrity, or stay committed to health can shape your journey profoundly. These friendships go beyond companionship; they become sources of direction and courage.

Purpose in Family

Family is often where we first learn about purpose, values, and resilience. Purposeful families are not defined merely by lineage or obligation but by a shared vision of life.

- In such families, purpose offers clarity during decision-making. Values such as honesty, respect, compassion, and hard work guide both parents and children, shaping an environment where individuals not only survive but thrive.
- Purpose also provides resilience in adversity. Families who see themselves as united by something greater than comfort—whether it is service, education, or spiritual growth—face challenges with greater solidarity.

Consider the life of Nelson Mandela.

His decades in prison were sustained not only by his own sense of mission but also by the purpose shared by his family and community, who carried forward the struggle for justice. Their shared purpose allowed them to endure unimaginable hardship and emerge stronger.

Additionally, purpose leaves a legacy in regular families. Integrity-driven parents instill principles in addition to wealth. Children raised in these kinds of settings are born with a compass that serves them well throughout their lives. Generational ripples are produced by families with a purpose.

Purpose in Community

Communities are where purpose grows into movements. When individuals come together around shared values, they create collective strength far beyond what they could achieve alone.

Communities gain resilience, trust, and a sense of belonging when they have purpose. It unites people despite differences in culture, religion, or class.

Purpose-aligned communities foster environments of compassion, collaboration, and advancement.

This fact is constantly demonstrated by history. The liberation struggle in India, the American civil rights movement, and grassroots environmental initiatives worldwide were all collective expressions of purpose as well as political undertakings.

Smaller-scale examples of purposeful communities include workplaces that stress moral behavior and well-being, neighborhoods that come together during times of crisis, and schools that place an equal emphasis on values and academics. These instances serve as a reminder that shared vision, not chance, is what makes communities thrive.

When people get together with the same goal, ripples become waves. A grassroots initiative that changed landscapes and gave women more power, Wangari Maathai's Green Belt Movement started with her dedication to reforestation. Similar to this, the Swachh Bharat Abhiyan in India flourished because people accepted personal accountability for maintaining cleanliness, transforming the initiative into a cultural shift.

The Ripple Effect: Living Your Purpose Inspires Others Around You

Purpose is never contained within the individual. It radiates outward, influencing others often in silent but profound ways. Just as a stone creates ripples across a lake, every act aligned with purpose affects people we may never meet.

Our greatest potent influence is frequently unsaid. Although people rarely recall what we say, they do observe the way we live. A teacher who exudes passion and patience can inspire students to be lifelong learners. A leader sets a new standard for their organization when they prioritize ethics over expediency. Gandhi influenced millions of people with his simplicity and discipline without asking for loyalty. Because his aim was genuine, it spread like wildfire.

The Global Ripple

In an interconnected world, purpose travels across borders. Greta Thunberg's solitary school strike sparked a global youth movement for climate action. One individual's clarity can now ripple into millions of lives through digital connectivity.

Living the Ripple

Purposeful influence is not reserved for the famous. Every small act: kindness, integrity, service, etc., creates ripples. We may never see their full impact, but each purposeful choice contributes to the greater fabric of humanity.

Families are where ripples are often most visible. Children absorb values not by instruction alone but by example. Parents who live with integrity, service, or resilience silently shape generations.

Ratan Tata's leadership in business and philanthropy reflects a family culture where service and ethics were central. His influence, in turn, has inspired countless entrepreneurs to see success as impact rather than profit. Purpose lived authentically becomes legacy.

To Sum it Up

Purpose is not only an internal compass but also a relational force. It transforms love into collaboration, friendship into growth, family into legacy, and community into collective power. Purpose lived authentically creates ripples that inspire others, reminding us that our lives are deeply interconnected.

To live with purpose is to recognize that we are both shapers and shaped by those we love, those who walk beside us, and the communities we belong to. Our choices today weave into the fabric of tomorrow, creating patterns that endure long after we are gone.

Exercise:

Reflecting on Purpose in Your Relationships

- **Shared Values:** In your closest relationships, what values do you notice in common? Where do you feel aligned, and where do you feel tension?
- **Ripple Awareness:** Recall a time when your actions positively influenced someone else. How did that experience affect your understanding of your purpose?
- **Relationship Growth:** Choose one relationship. How could you bring more purpose into this bond—through deeper listening, shared goals, or living by values?
- **Legacy of Influence:** If someone close to you were asked, "What do they stand for?"—what would they say? Does that align with your own vision of purpose?
- **Future Intentions:** What is one step you can take this week to live with more purpose in your relationships—whether with a loved one, a friend, or your community?

Chapter 8

Living a Purposeful Life

The Journey So Far

As we arrive at this final chapter, it is worth pausing to look back at the journey we have traveled together.

- **In the earlier chapters of this book, we have explored life from many angles,** each one important, each one shaping the way we live and grow. We began with the idea of purpose, the inner compass that gives meaning to our lives. We saw how purpose, once discovered and nurtured, can bring clarity to decisions and resilience to struggles.
- **After that, we examined success and discovered that it is determined by how well our activities reflect our underlying ideals** rather than just by material wealth, notoriety, or recognition. We looked at money and saw that it may be a tool if we use it for a purpose, but it can also be a slave if we approach it as the end objective. Relationships become deeper and more rewarding when they are based on shared meaning, service, and authenticity rather than superficial expectations.
- **We also looked at resilience, progress, and self-awareness,** how serving others connects us to something greater than ourselves, how introspection helps us harmonize our inner and outward worlds, and how setbacks can become stepping stones. All of these realizations combined to create an image of a life that

is not only lived on a daily basis but rather one that is purposeful, fulfilling, and directed.

We now tie everything together in this final chapter. This chapter focuses on integration rather than adding something new.

It shows how purpose may permeate every area of life and serve as the cornerstone of our daily lives. Knowing that every decision, every relationship, every objective, and every obstacle is a part of a greater journey is what it means to live a purposeful life.

Being purposeful does not equate to being flawless. It entails leading an aligned life. It entails establishing routines that keep us focused on what really matters and getting up each morning with clarity, even in the face of uncertainty. It also entails realizing that meaning is a lifelong adventure that changes as we mature, gain knowledge, and make contributions rather than a single, definitive finding.

To illustrate these truths, we will turn once again to the lives of two extraordinary individuals: Dr. A.P.J. Abdul Kalam, India's "People's President," who lived with simplicity, service, and vision, and Oprah Winfrey, the global media leader and philanthropist, who transformed personal pain into a worldwide mission of empowerment.

Their stories remind us that purpose is not reserved for a chosen few—it is available to anyone willing to live with courage, gratitude, and intention.

Integration of Purpose Across All Aspects of Life

Purpose is like light; it has to shine into every corner of our lives.

If it is confined to one area, such as work or personal ambition, it creates an imbalance. A truly purposeful life integrates meaning into relationships, work, health, community, and spirituality.

1. Purpose in Relationships

Relationships are the heart of life. They are the spaces where we give and receive love, where we grow, where we face our greatest challenges, and where we find our deepest joys. A purposeful person approaches relationships not as transactions, but as sacred connections. They see relationships as opportunities to nurture, uplift, and learn.

Dr. A.P.J. Abdul Kalam never married or had children, but his relationships with his students, colleagues, and citizens of India were deeply meaningful.

He saw himself as a mentor and guide, constantly encouraging young people to dream big and serve their country. His purpose was not tied to a private family but to a national one—he became, in many ways, the "father" of millions of young Indians.

Oprah Winfrey, by contrast, grew up in an environment where relationships often brought pain. Her early childhood was marked by abuse and instability. Yet, as she grew, she chose not to let these experiences define her relationships. Instead, she built connections rooted in authenticity and healing. Through her talk shows, interviews, and foundation, she created spaces where people could share their stories, feel seen, and find strength.

Her purpose transformed her relationships into sources of empowerment for millions.

Relationships become about growth, service, and connection when purpose is included; they no longer revolve around possession or control.

2. Purpose in Work

Our lives are mostly consumed by work. Even achievement might feel meaningless when it is divorced from purpose. Even difficulties have value when they are in line with a purpose.

Kalam never saw labor as a means to an end. Although he was actively involved in India's space and missile projects as a scientist, his overarching goal was always to see India become powerful, independent, and well-respected globally.

His unwavering commitment to his endeavors was driven by a strong feeling of national service as well as ambition. His efforts as president later shifted to empowering young people and creating a future vision for India.

For Oprah, her job was about transformation as much as entertainment.

She recognized early in her profession that she had a talent for establishing a deeper connection with individuals. She started talking about self-belief, healing, and resilience by using her television platform to convey stories that mattered. Her program touched lives and became a cultural force in addition to being a ratings triumph.

Work with a purpose adds vitality, satisfaction, and influence. It turns careers into legacies and jobs into callings.

3. Purpose in Health

Although it is fundamental, health is frequently disregarded when discussing purpose. Even the most admirable goals cannot be achieved without physical and mental health. Purpose-driven health is about treating the body and mind as vehicles of our mission, not about image or perfection.

Kalam led a modest, orderly existence. He led a balanced lifestyle, ate modestly, and abstained from excess. He was able to work long hours well into his nineties because of this simplicity. His health practices were aimed at maintaining his capacity to serve, not at indulgence.

- Oprah has a distinct health journey. For decades, she battled body image and weight. However, she reframed these difficulties as a part of her life's journey rather than viewing them as failures.
- She enabled millions of people to face their own health issues without embarrassment by being transparent about her experiences. Her mission turned her own hardships into lessons for the whole.

Maintaining your health while living a worthwhile life entails taking care of others as well as yourself.

4. Purpose in Community and Service

The deepest expression of purpose is found in service. A purpose that is limited to the ego is still unfinished.

Service characterized Kalam's life. Whether he worked in education, leadership, or science, his goal was always to uplift others. Serving until his dying breath, he was still lecturing kids in his final moments.

Oprah has also made service the core of her mission.

She has made it possible for others to succeed through her generosity, particularly through the Oprah Winfrey Leadership Academy for Girls in South Africa. Her work is about empowerment and transformation, not just charity.

Purpose in community reminds us that our lives are not just about what we achieve, but about what we give.

5. Purpose in Spirituality

We are connected to something more than ourselves through spirituality. It is the source of inner strength and tranquility.

Kalam believed that faith and humility were the foundations of spirituality.

He was a devoted Muslim who frequently cited the Bible and believed that spirituality and science could coexist. He felt that significant external accomplishments required a robust inner existence.

Spirituality served as the cornerstone of Oprah's subsequent work.

She frequently talks about hearing the "still, little voice within," which she refers to as the spirit's or God's voice. She was able to maintain her composure in the face of fame, fortune, and difficulties thanks to her spiritual foundation.

A purposeful life embraces spirituality not as dogma but as a connection to God, to humanity, to the universe, and to one's higher self.

Daily Practices That Anchor Purpose

Purpose is not sustained by big visions alone. It needs daily practices that keep us grounded. Three of the most powerful are gratitude, reflection, and intentional planning.

1. Gratitude

Gratitude shifts our focus from scarcity to abundance. It allows us to appreciate what we have, even as we strive for more.

Kalam often spoke about the teachers and mentors who shaped his life. His gratitude was not just words; it was expressed in how he honored their teachings and passed them on to others.

Oprah is famous for promoting gratitude journaling.

She has often said that writing down five things she is grateful for each day transformed her life. This simple practice is one reason she has been able to stay grounded despite immense success.

Gratitude keeps us aligned with purpose by reminding us of the blessings that fuel our journey.

2. Reflection

Reflection is how experience becomes wisdom. Without it, we risk repeating mistakes or losing direction.

Kalam reflected through writing.

His books, like Wings of Fire and Ignited Minds, are not just records of events but reflections on meaning and vision.

Oprah uses conversation as a reflection.

Through her interviews, she not only helps others reflect but also deepens her own understanding of life.

Reflection allows us to pause, learn, and adjust our path toward greater alignment with purpose.

3. Intentional Planning

Purpose without action remains a dream. Intentional planning bridges the gap between vision and execution.

Kalam was meticulous in planning his work. Every project, every schedule, was approached with clarity and discipline. His intentionality ensured that his vision translated into results.

Oprah is equally deliberate. Ending her talk show at its peak and moving into new ventures was not impulsive; it was intentional, aligned with her evolving sense of purpose.

Intentional planning turns purpose into reality.

Purpose as a Lifelong Journey

Perhaps the most important truth about purpose is that it is not a one-time discovery. It evolves with us.

Kalam once dreamed of being a pilot. When that did not happen, his purpose shifted to aeronautical engineering and later to national service. Eventually, he became a teacher and mentor. At every stage, his purpose grew with him.

Oprah's journey, too, reflects evolution. From a young girl overcoming abuse, to a talk-show host, to a media leader, to a spiritual teacher and philanthropist—her purpose has expanded continuously.

Purpose is not fixed. It is a journey. At different stages, it may look different, but it is always guiding us forward.

Practical Exercises

Gratitude Journal:– Write five things you are grateful for daily.

Ask yourself-

- What moments in my life have felt most meaningful?
- Where am I living in alignment with my values?
- Where am I drifting away?

Life Integration Wheel: (Diagram to be added) Rate work, relationships, health, community, and spirituality on how aligned they are with your purpose.

Intentional Weekly Planning: (Calendar for eg, to be added) Each week, set three purposeful intentions and review them at week's end.

Purpose Evolution Journal: Reflect on how your sense of purpose has changed over time.

Purpose as the Compass

Living a purposeful life is not about perfection. It is about integration, daily grounding, and lifelong growth. It is about seeing challenges as part of the journey, relationships as sacred, work as service, health as stewardship, and spirituality as connection.

The lives of A.P.J. Abdul Kalam and Oprah Winfrey remind us that purpose can be lived in many forms, through service, teaching, storytelling, or empowerment—but its essence remains the same: to live with alignment, intention, and contribution.

Chapter 9

Walking Forward with Purpose

As you close this book, remember: purpose is not a destination. It is a compass.

A destination is fixed, you reach it, and the journey ends. But a compass never stops working. It is there with you when you wake each morning, quietly pointing toward what matters most. It will guide you when you are uncertain, correct you when you drift, and evolve with you as you grow.

When we began this journey, we asked a simple yet profound question: What does it mean to live with purpose? Through each chapter, we uncovered that purpose is not something you stumble upon in a single moment of revelation. Rather, it is something you cultivate, refine, and embody across every aspect of life.

You have seen how purpose influences the way you think about success, moving from external validation to inner fulfillment. You have explored how it transforms your relationship with money, shifting it from being a master that controls you to a servant that supports your highest values. You have witnessed how purpose strengthens relationships, giving them depth, resilience, and authenticity. You have discovered how resilience itself is born when you anchor yourself in something larger than your pain. You have reflected on how self-awareness sharpens your inner compass, allowing you to see clearly who you are and what you stand for. And you have learned that service, acts of kindness, and contribution, both big and small, expand your life far beyond its own boundaries.

All these lessons are not separate; they are threads in a larger fabric. When woven together, they form the pattern of a purposeful life.

But how do you live such a life?

The answer is simple, though not always easy. You live purposefully through daily practices.

Gratitude, reflection, and intentional planning may seem ordinary, but it is in these ordinary choices that extraordinary lives are built. A moment of gratitude can soften a heart. A few minutes of reflection can bring clarity in chaos. A small intentional choice can redirect the course of an entire life.

Living with purpose does not mean you will never stumble. Even the most purposeful lives face setbacks, doubts, and detours. What matters is that you return to your compass, again and again. Purpose is not about being perfect; it is about being aligned.

Think of the great examples we explored. Dr. A.P.J. Abdul Kalam, born into a modest family in Rameswaram, carried his dreams into the laboratories of ISRO and DRDO, and later into the office of the President of India.

He faced rejection, obstacles, and failures, but he never lost sight of his compass: service to the nation through science, education, and inspiration. His life reminds us that purpose transforms even humble beginnings into legacies that touch millions.

On the other side of the world, Oprah Winfrey turned her personal struggles: poverty, abuse, and self-doubt, into a mission of empowerment.

She did not arrive at her purpose in one dramatic moment, but through years of evolving, experimenting, failing, and learning. Her compass pointed toward lifting others, giving voice to the voiceless, and spreading healing. That compass guided her to build not only a career, but a legacy of transformation that continues to ripple across the world.

Your story, too, holds the same potential.

It may not look like Kalam's or Oprah's, but it carries its own unique resonance.

Every step you take, no matter how small, becomes part of a greater story. A kind word to a stranger, an act of integrity in a difficult moment, a choice to live in alignment with your values—these are not trivial. They are the brushstrokes of your life's masterpiece.

And remember this: your story is never just your own. Purpose ripples outward. It touches your family, your community, your workplace, and sometimes even people you may never meet.

You may not always see the impact, but it is there. Just as a seed planted today becomes a tree that shades future generations, the choices you make now create a legacy far beyond your lifetime.

So as you set this book down, carry forward this truth: Purpose is both the map and the journey. It is not a finish line waiting for you at the end of the road. It is the way you walk the road itself. It is the courage to choose meaning over convenience, alignment over compromise, and contribution over indifference.

When your story is told, it will not be the trophies or possessions that define you, but the impact you made, the love you gave, and the meaning you created. That is the measure of a purposeful life.

And that story, woven from your choices, your struggles, and your acts of love, will ultimately become the legacy you leave behind.

Continue the Journey

The Why Code is just the beginning.

Your real transformation starts from within.

Discover programs, coaching, and conscious leadership journeys at:

www.enrisewithin.com

Scan the QR code to explore:

Purpose & clarity programs

1:1 personal coaching

Leadership & mindful living journeys

Rise. Align. Lead. Live with Purpose.